GRA
THEATRE

presents

WHITER
THAN SNOW

by Mike Kenny

First performance

New Wolsey Theatre, Ipswich

5 March 2009

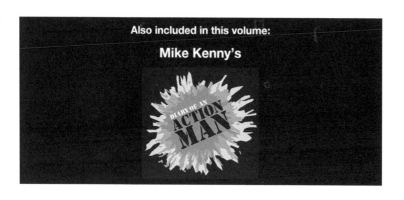

Also included in this volume:

Mike Kenny's

DIARY OF AN
**ACTION
MAN**

Credits

Cast

In order of speaking

Frieda **Kiruna Stamell**
Otto **Nick Read**
Bertha **Sarah Bennett**
Little Otto **Milton Lopes**
Sam/Regina **Tom Thomasson**
Vera, the Family Sign Language Interpreter **Jude Mahon**
Eirwen / Soldier **Esther McAuley**

Creative Team

Writer **Mike Kenny**
Director **Jenny Sealey**
Assistant to the Director **Jeni Draper**
Design **Marc Laine**
Lighting Design **Richard G Jones**
Sound Design **Ivan Stott**
Voice Coach **Christopher Holt**
Choreographer **Athina Valha**

Production Team

Production Manager **Simon Sturgess**
Company Stage Manager **Patricia Davenport**
Technical Stage Manager **Chloe Kenward**
Access Workers **Wayne 'Pickles' Norman, Rachel Drazek**

Workshop Team

David Ellington
Willie Elliott
Alison Halstead
Karina Jones
Karen Spicer
Samantha Tatlow

Thanks

The Unicorn Theatre, Andy Beardmore, Neil Francis, Dr Michael Wright,
The People Show, Milorad Zakula, Caroline Hetherington, Dr Jane Barnard and
Nickie Wildin.

In the original tour the part of Little Otto was played by **James O'Driscoll**.

A note from the Writer

These two plays emerge from a conversation I've been having with Jenny Sealey. It began in the 80s when we met in Leeds at Red Ladder to work on a play. Jenny was then an actor. I had only recently begun my career as a playwright. We sat down as a company of white and British Asian, hearing and deaf people and we wanted to make a play that would speak to as wide an audience as possible. I suppose the word we tend to use is accessibility, but I think I prefer universality. Our conversation has continued through work with Interplay, Fittings Multimedia Arts and, latterly, Graeae. Each play is a sign post on the way. It's where we've got up to. We keep making discoveries. We never get a single right answer. The conversation is not exclusive. It has involved many other people along the way. It has influenced all of my work, not only with Graeae, but with other companies too. These two plays are good examples of the variety of questions which come up and the different answers too.

Whiter Than Snow

The inspiration for this play was a short newspaper article headlined 'A Shortage of Dwarfs'. It was supposed to be a joke. It didn't say much except that there were so many productions of *Snow White* that Christmas that theatres were having trouble finding casts.

I thought I'd like to look at this from the point of view of the performers so I began writing about a family of short stature when I found that there had been such a family. I came across the Ovitz family, seven brothers and sisters who called themselves the Lilliput Troupe and performed in eastern Europe during the second world war. Their real story was an inspiration. It took them from Transylvania, through Auschwitz and eventually to Israel. I recommend it. It's extraordinary, but this is not it. This goes off in various other directions. It's a fiction.

Originally this piece was a commission for Birmingham REP but I involved Graeae very early in the process as the obvious partner and it quickly emerged that I was leading us into a new area.

I had never written a piece that looked at a specific disability before. Universal access on the basis of talent and ability, not disability, is a good principle, but our central family were short and therefore had to be played by short actors. There are some things you just can't act – aren't there? Actually all this stuff got written into the play. It was another of those stops on the way in a conversation that has been going on for twenty years now and shows no sign of stopping.

Mike Kenny 2009

A note from the Director

The Play

Whiter then Snow is a retelling of Snow White from the perspective of a family of short stature. Genetics, eugenics and cloning are placed within the Snow White fairytale. The Frantz family, who are people of short stature, meet Snow White who has been cloned by her mother. Snow White's mother is an esteemed geneticist in pursuit of perfection. As the family try to grasp the complexity of perfection in a world where they are seen as freaks, the play becomes a battlefield to prevent science from ridding the world of short people, but at the same time it understands that science, if used wisely, can be of benefit. With an unexpected twist, the play reveals the necessity of choice of what we perceive to be perfect or imperfect, and highlights our differences and uniqueness.

The play allows young people to engage creatively, intellectually and emotionally with the characters' journeys and observe for themselves the decisions that are made at the end.

The Style

The cast of six disabled actors and a Sign Language Interpreter set up the play through telling the story of what had happened to them. This style allows the characters to describe the action and say who is playing who so that a Blind and Visually Impaired audience can access the story and action. The Sign Language Interpreter is a family member so she is always around signing what the characters are saying and also giving a deaf audience some of her thoughts and comments.

The style of a play within a play is always challenging but the panto element allows us chaos and fun amid the landscape of war.

The set design was made so the family could live underneath and perform on top. The moving of the set into a different formation is linked to them always having to move away from trouble.

Biographies

Mike Kenny Writer

Mike, who grew up on the Welsh border, found himself an actor/teacher in Leeds Playhouse Theatre in Education in the late 70s. He devised theatre with the company for nine years. After leaving, he freelanced as an actor in theatre and TV, but worked increasingly in writing for children's theatre companies. He became a writer when funding cuts meant companies could no longer devise work in-house. Also, his eldest son, then seven, became school-phobic leading to the subject matter of his first play for the very young, *The Lost Child*.

Mike sees fairy tales as the real myths of childhood. He feels like he is often rescuing them from the thick layers of sentiment that have obscured them over the years, and returning them to their original power. Recent work includes *Walking the Tightrope* for the under fives; an adaptation of *Of Mice and Men* for Mind the…Gap; *Fittings: The Last Freakshow* for Graeae and Fittings Multimedia Arts and *The Railway Children* at the National Railway Museum with a real steam train.

Mike's award-winning plays include: *Sink or Swim,* Time Out Best Children's Play 1995; *Stepping Stones*, Writer's Guild Best Children's Play 1997; *Diary of an Action Man*, Time Out Best Children's Play 2003. He was the first ever recipient of The Children's Award from Arts Council England for playwriting, and in 2002 his work with Mind the…Gap received the TMA/Stage Award for Special Contribution to Regional Theatre. In 2003 he was included by The Independent on Sunday on a list of Top Ten Living UK Playwrights.

Jenny Sealey Director

Jenny's directing career started with a Calouste Gulbenkian Director Training Bursary with Interplay Theatre Company. There she co-directed *Sea Changes*, *Stepping Stones* and *Mad Meg*. In 1997 her reputation for devising signed plays for deaf audiences and creating multisensory theatre led her to become Graeae's Artistic Director.

All productions are fuelled by a passion to find a new theatrical voice which explores how the aesthetics of access (sign language and audio description, diverse physicality and differing voices) can be integral to a production.

Graeae productions include *The Fall of the House of Usher* adapted by Steven Berkoff; *Fittings: The Last Freakshow* by Mike Kenny; *The Changeling* adapted by Clare McIntyre; *peeling* by Kaite O'Reilly; *Diary of an Action Man* by Mike Kenny; *On Blindness* by Glyn Cannon; *Bent* by Martin Sherman and *Blasted* by Sarah Kane.

Recent co-productions include: *Flower Girls* by Richard Cameron with New Wolsey Theatre, Ipswich; *Static* by Dan Rebellato with Suspect Culture and new street arts venture *The Medal Ceremony* with Australian performers, Strange Fruit.

Freelance work includes *Signs of a Diva* and *The Alexandras*. She lives with her partner Danny Braverman and their son Jonah. Jenny was recently awarded an MBE for services to disability arts.

Kiruna Stamell Frieda

Kiruna made her acting debut in Baz Luhrmann's *Moulin Rouge* in 2000. Since then she has performed with the Sydney Theatre Company in *Macbeth* and across Europe with Victoria/Contact Theatre. Most recently you may have seen Kiruna on the BBC in *EastEnders* playing the role of Mrs Fielding; in the series *All The Small Things* and in *The Choir*.

If you could play any character, who would it be?

"I have always wanted to play an ordinary character in a soap. I like Mrs Fielding (in EastEnders), because the character is about what she does... we aren't preoccupied with her height, yet obviously it's there all the time. To be in a mainstream soap, even only occasionally, is a huge boon to me. It acknowledges that slowly the barriers around disability are slowly breaking down and the mainstream is opening up. But who I really want to play.... That's easy... I have always always wanted to be Dr Who's Assistant... I am a very easy traveller."

Nick Read Otto

Nick was born in St Albans, Hertfordshire. After leaving school at the age of 16 he entered into the exciting world of show biz. He has appeared in many different roles from promotions in the dingiest night club to being on the big screen and is enjoying every second of it.

If you could play any character, who would it be?

"I would love to play a psychotic villain, as the character would be easy to get into. I really like Heath Ledger's portrayal of The Joker."

Sarah Bennett Bertha

Watford-born and bred, Sarah's first job was as an Ewok in the film *The Return of the Jedi*. Since then she has appeared in films and adverts in many guises. She has completed fifteen *Snow White* pantomime seasons and many corporate events. She has dabbled in television and motion-capture for animation. Sarah says the best thing is meeting so many diverse people along the way.

If you could play any character, who would you it be?

"One of *The Borrowers*. How much fun could you have sending people crazy, moving their stuff around?!"

Milton Lopes Little Otto

Milton was born in Cape Verde and lived in Portugal most of his life. He began his acting career in Lisbon in 1998 and since then he has worked in Mexico, Scotland, England, Angola and France, acting in theatre, television and film. He worked for Graeae for the first time in 2004 in *Bent*. He now lives in London.

If you could play any character, who would it be?

"*The Count Of Monte Cristo*. He has faith that transforms him from a unfairly punished man to one of the richest in the world. He is the most intelligent character that ever existed, planning every step that he takes in order to realise his goals."

Tom Thomasson Sam/Regina

Tom trained at the University of Reading. He has toured with Graeae in their previous run of *Whiter Than Snow* and in *Static.* He also works as a freelance drama facilitator and has delivered workshops for companies including Kazzum Arts and Diverse City. He is part of the pool of tutors for Half Moon Theatre Company and Eastside Educational Trust.

If you could play any character, who would it be?

"Dr Who, or Marty McFly from the *Back to the Future* films. I love the varied and eccentric storylines that encompass science fiction – more importantly, it's just so flipping cool to have a time machine! I want one please."

Jude Mahon Vera, the Family Sign Language Interpreter

Jude has worked with Graeae for several years as a Sign Language Interpreter and performer. She trained at Mountview Academy of Theatre Arts as an actress which led to roles in theatre and television. After securing a place in the final of *Funny Women Stand-up Comedy Awards* Jude can now be seen making people laugh on London's comedy circuit.

If you could play any character, who would it be?

"Eliza Doolittle in *My Fair Lady* but instead of a cockney accent, I'd have a harsh Warrington twang!"

Esther McAuley Eirwen

Esther graduated from Mountview Academy of Theatre Arts, where she won the 2005 Sir John Gielgud Bursary Award. Theatre credits include: The Sam Wanamaker Festival, Globe Theatre; *Pills Thrills & Automobiles*, Ape Theatre Company; *The Emperor Jones*, National Theatre; *A Midsummer Night's Dream*, *Theatre Delicatessen*, *Wild Honey, Habeas Corpus*, *She Stoops to Conquer*, and *Arcadia* in rep at Pitlochry Festival Theatre. Short films include: *Remembering Love*; *NYFA*, *Sweet Sorrow*; *Joker's Pack*.

If you could play any character, who would it be?

"Matilda Wormwood from Roald Dahl's *Matilda*. I would have to work on my 'psychokinetic' powers to do the role justice. If I could move heavy furniture and buckets of slime using only my will power, there would be scenes of confused and very slimy looking bullies trapped between banisters, in shelving units, and industrial sized sinks, all over London."

Marc Laine Designer

Marc graduated from the Ecole Nationale Supriéure des Arts-Décoratifs in 2000. He has been working since then for theatre and opera, mostly in France. Last year he designed, among other projects, the sets for: *Albert Herring* by Benjamin Britten, at the Opera Comique in Paris; *Kiss Me Quick*, at the Theatre de la Bastille (Paris Autumn Festival); *Alice* by Lewis Carroll, at the Ferme du Buisson Bastille (Paris Autumn Festival).

Ivan Stott Sound Design

Ivan has worked in theatre professionally for 20 years as a Composer, Sound Designer, Songwriter, Actor and Workshop Facilitator. His recent work includes *The Snow Queen* (West Yorkshire Playhouse), *Lysistrata* (Dundee Rep), *The Little Mermaid* (Honolulu Tenney Theater, Hawaii, USA), *We're Going on a Bear Hunt* (Polka Theatre, London), *Death of a Salesman* (Octagon Theatre Bolton), *The Trial* (York Theatre Royal), *Hue Boy, Silly Billy, The Girl Who Lost Her Smile, Jack* (Tutti Frutti Productions).

Richard G Jones Lighting Designer

Richard designed the lighting for *Sweeney Todd* at the Eugene O'Neill Theatre in New York, for which he won The Drama Desk Award for Outstanding Lighting. He has recently been nominated for a TMA award for best lighting design for *The Railway Children* at the National Railway Museum in York. Richard has recently designed the lighting for, amongst others, *Horrid Henry Live and Horrid!* at the Trafalgar Studios, *Sunset Boulevard* at the Comedy Theatre, *Ich war noch niemals in New York* at the Operettanhaus in Hamburg and *Celebrating Christmas with the Salvation Army* at the Royal Albert Hall.

Jeni Draper Assistant to the Director

A seasoned actor and BSL interpreter, Jeni has enjoyed working with Graeae on many productions – most recently performing in *Static* at Soho Theatre. She has also added directing to her CV with *Counting the Ways* at the Millfield Theatre for Face Front Inclusive Theatre which will tour later in 2009.

Christopher Holt Voice Coach

Christopher has a BA in Performing Arts from Middlesex Polytechnic and an MA in Theatre (Directing) from the Royal Holloway University of London. For 15 years he was an actor and singer appearing in national and international work including musicals, operas and plays. Christopher is now a freelance theatre director, voice and acting coach and a Senior Lecturer in Theatre Studies and Performing Arts at London Metropolitan University.

Athina Vahla Choreographer

Athina is a multidisciplinary independent artist specialising in choreography. Her work is largely site-specific movement in historical buildings. She works internationally both as a teacher and creator and is an Artsadmin Associate Artist.

Simon Sturgess Production Manager

Simon is a freelance Production Manager whose recent work includes *La Cage Aux Folles* at the Playhouse Theatre and *Come Dancing* and *Hansel and Gretel* both at Theatre Royal Stratford East. Simon's previous work with Graeae includes *Blasted*, *Diary of an Action Man*, *On Blindness* and *Peeling*.

Patricia Davenport Stage Manager

Patricia has recently company-managed Kneehigh's *Brief Encounter* and stage managed Red Earth's *Cinderella's Sisters*. Patricia is ecstatic to be working with Graeae again.

Chloe Kenward Technical Stage Manager

Chloe has worked as a lighting designer, touring re-lighter and technician throughout North America and Europe for companies including Headlong, Vincent Dance Theatre, The National Theatre, Peepolykus and Quicksilver.

Wayne 'Pickles' Norman Access Worker

Wayne spent over 30 years, man and boy as an actor, including the Artful Dodger in the West End, *Worzel Gummidge*, *Grange Hill*, *Inspector Morse* and *Doctor Who*. And for nearly 20 years he has been a leader of a disabled Scout troupe. He has been working with Graeae for the past 7 years as an Access Support Worker and occasional driver and gardener.

Rachel Drazek Access Worker

Rachel works as an Access Worker for a number of companies, and has also trained as an actress. She is delighted to be involved with *Whiter than Snow*, and grateful for the variety of experiences this job offers. She's interested to be backstage for a while!

Original Co-producer for *Whiter Than Snow*

Birmingham Repertory Theatre

Birmingham Repertory Theatre is one of Britain's leading national producing theatre companies. From its base in Birmingham, The REP produces over twenty new productions each year.

The commissioning and production of new work lies at the core of The REP's programme. The Door was established ten years ago as a theatre dedicated to the production and presentation of new writing. In this time, it has given world premieres to new plays from a new generation of British playwrights.

Developing new and particularly younger audiences is also at the heart of The REP's work, in its various education initiatives, such as Transmissions, The Young REP, REP's Children, as well as with the programming of work in The Door for children.

The REP's productions regularly transfer to London and tour nationally and internationally.

Artistic Director **Rachel Kavanaugh**
Executive Director **Stuart Rogers**

GRAEae
THEATRE COMPANY

Graeae is a world leader in developing and promoting disabled-led theatre for a diverse audience. With over 28 years' experience, the company is now uniquely positioned to showcase the excellence of disabled artists. From our new home in Hackney to venues and audiences across the UK and beyond, we are positioning ourselves at the heart of the Cultural Olympiad in the run up to 2012. Despite progress, both legislative and cultural, and slowly shifting attitudes, there remains a lack of recognition of the talents of disabled people in the arts. Our programme of work seeks to address this through our productions, education and outreach projects and our commitment to training the next generation of directors, performers and writers.

Graeae's Vision

To create a new dramatic language that demolishes the barriers to the performance and appreciation of theatre.

Strategic aims

- **World-class theatre:** creating and touring high quality, high impact theatre that is unmistakably Graeae's, providing a platform for the skill, vision and excellence of disabled artists
- **Training and education:** creating a programme of inclusive training and education activities which engages, inspires and nurtures emerging and professional disabled artists
- **Championing accessibility:** creating, operating, supporting and advising on accessible environments and practice

Graeae

Artistic Director/CEO **Jenny Sealey**
Executive Director/CEO **Judith Kilvington**
General Manager **Kevin Walsh**
Finance Manager **Kudzai Mushangwe**
Training & Learning Projects Manager **Rachel Bagshaw**
Literary Manager **Alex Bulmer**
Access Coordinators **Sharon Payne** and **Michael Achtman**
Administrative Assistant **Victoria Stevens**
Management Support Worker **Carissa Hope Lynch**
Training & Learning Projects Assistant **Dan McGowan and Laura Martin Simpson**
Marketing Officer for *Whiter Than Snow* **Mark Waddell**
Press Manager for *Whiter Than Snow* **Anne Mayer**
Graphic Design **Stem Design**

Board of Directors
Steve Mannix (Chair), Emma Dunton, Avis Johns, Judith Mellor, Steve Moffitt, Jodi Myers, Theresa Veith.

Associate Artists
Jamie Beddard, Mandy Colleran, David Ellington, Tim Gebbels, Kaz Langley, Radha Manjeshwar, Nicola Miles-Wildin, Sophie Partridge, Nicole Stoute, Amit Sharma, Donal Toolan, David Toole.

WHITER

THAN SNOW

First published in 2009 by Oberon Books Ltd
521 Caledonian Road, London N7 9RH
Tel: 020 7607 3637 / Fax: 020 7607 3629
e-mail: info@oberonbooks.com
www.oberonbooks.com

A catalogue record for this book is available from the British
Library.

ISBN: 978-1-84002-918-5

Cover image Robert Day. Graphics Stem Design and Eureka!

Printed in Great Britain by CPI Antony Rowe Ltd, Chippenham.

Characters

FRIEDA FRANTZ
Teenager. Person of restricted growth.

OTTO FRANTZ
Frieda's father. Actor Manager. Irascible, slightly
self-deluding. Person of restricted growth.

BERTHA FRANTZ
Frieda's mother. Long-suffering. Person of
restricted growth.

LITTLE OTTO
Frieda's brother. Young, growing.

SAM
Stage manager. Very, very loyal to the Frantz
family. Secretly in love with Frieda.

VERA
The family Sign Language Interpreter.

EIRWEN
A clone, escaped.

REGINA
A scientist.

ERIC
A soldier.

Stage directions are in italic and are not to be spoken.

*The characters REGINA and the SOLDIER are played by different
actors at different points.*

13

Part One

A large empty stage, with a small figure in it.

The sound of distant gun fire.

FRIEDA   Once upon a time
On a very wide stage
Stands a young woman
Once upon a time
In a far away land
In a time of war
Stands a young woman.
Because you don't know her yet, or anything about her, you'll be noticing one thing about her and probably only one.
I'm short.

She pauses.

Have a good look
You have my permission.
OK?
Now get over it.
This is our story.

Scene One. The Biggest Littlest Show in the World introduce themselves.

OTTO   Time's money, Frieda. Come on, shift yourself.

FRIEDA   (*To audience.*) That's my father.
Otto Frantz. He's short.

OTTO   Biggest Littlest Show in the World. You'll have heard of us. We're very big round here.

BERTHA   (*Enters.*) Was that a joke?

OTTO   (*To audience.*) That's my wife.

FRIEDA   (*To audience.*) And my mother.
Bertha Frantz. She is short.

15

BERTHA	(*To audience.*) My husband thinks he's funny.
OTTO	Oh, lighten up.
FRIEDA	In those days we would turn up in a town and set up for the show.
OTTO	Ladies and Gentlemen, boys and girls For your pleasure and delight we'll be performing Snow White and the Seven Dwarfs.
FRIEDA	There wasn't actually seven.
OTTO	No, but that's the story. Snow White and the Seven…
FRIEDA	There were four.
OTTO	But the story…
FRIEDA	Three of them got a better offer.
OTTO	More money maybe.
FRIEDA	In a circus. Falling over.
OTTO	It's funny.
FRIEDA	It's easy.
OTTO	Not as easy as it looks. (*Falls, or trips.*) Years of practice. Now can I carry on?
BERTHA	You usually do.
LITTLE OTTO	Dad, can I talk to you about something?
BERTHA	(*To audience.*) My son, Little Otto.
FRIEDA	And my brother.
LITTLE OTTO	Also short.
FRIEDA	Sometimes.
LITTLE OTTO	We'll explain later. Dad.
OTTO	(*To LITTLE OTTO.*) Not now.

LITTLE OTTO	I've got an idea for the show.
BERTHA	You've got enough to do helping me. We've got all the costumes to iron or the Princess will look like a wreck.
LITTLE OTTO	He won't listen.
BERTHA	He doesn't do listening.
LITTLE OTTO	So it all started when we arrived at a small town.
OTTO	This place is going to be good for us. I can feel it in my bones.
SAM	Where are we again?
FRIEDA	(*To audience.*) Sam, the stage manager. He's tall.
OTTO	Get a move on, we've got a show to do. Where's Lucretia?
FRIEDA	Lucretia plays Snow White.
OTTO	She's beautiful. You'll love her.
SAM	She's not here yet.
FRIEDA	Sam. Are you going to say hallo?
SAM	I'm just the stage manager. Nobody talks to the stage manager.
FRIEDA	He's not as bad as he likes to appear.
OTTO	Times are hard, but what a show. Starring the lovely Lucretia Bolero as Snow White, and the Frantz family dwarfs including the shortest man in the world. Tell them Bertha.
BERTHA	Well you just have.
OTTO	But who is he?
BERTHA	I can't think, Otto.

OTTO | Me, it's me, woman. The shortest. Me.
(*To audience.*) Here tonight.
Bring your friends.

FRIEDA | And I'm Frieda Frantz.
So
That's everybody.

VERA | What about me?

FRIEDA | This is Vera.

VERA | I'm the family sign language interpreter.
Tall, very pretty, dark hair, etc.

FRIEDA | So
Once upon a time
In a far away land
In a time of war
We came to a town do a show
This is the story of what happened

EIRWEN | (*Enters.*) And what about me?

FRIEDA | You, my dear Eirwen, were, at this point in the story, sitting outside in a car.

EIRWEN | Cold.

FRIEDA | Yes.

EIRWEN | Shivering.

FRIEDA | Yes.

EIRWEN | So get a move on.

FRIEDA | We're trying
That's when it all started.
When she arrived.

EIRWEN | Thank you.

FRIEDA | And much to my dismay, you didn't come alone.
Scene Two. Two Strangers arrive.
Dad.

EIRWEN	Firstly, this soldier came in. His name was Eric.
LITTLE OTTO	In this scene Dad will play the part of the soldier. Go up the ladder to look tall.
EIRWEN	He's tall and unfriendly.
OTTO	Okay then, Eric climbs the ladder in a tall and unfriendly manner.
LITTLE OTTO	Lovely. He said.
SOLDIER	I'm looking for Mr Otto Frantz, general manager of The Biggest Smallest Show in the World.
FRIEDA	At this point we had no idea who he was.
EIRWEN	And with him was a woman.
LITTLE OTTO	My mum will play the part of the woman. Mum!
BERTHA	You mean Regina?
LITTLE OTTO	Yes. You be Regina. Put on these glasses and climb the ladder.
BERTHA	No.
LITTLE OTTO	You'll have to.
BERTHA	I don't want to.
EIRWEN	It's a good part.
BERTHA	I know it's a good part, but no.
LITTLE OTTO	Why not?
BERTHA	I don't like heights. Don't look at me like that. Oh alright. Regina climbs the ladder. Cautiously.
FRIEDA	Don't look down.

BERTHA	Don't worry, I won't.
EIRWEN	Her name was Regina Woolf.
FRIEDA	The woman looked around The room seemed to get colder And she said. To the soldier.
REGINA	Eric, why on earth have we stopped here? It's late, it's cold and we're in the middle of nowhere.
FRIEDA	She was nearly as tall. And very, very strange.
SOLDIER	I'm under orders to see someone. It won't take long. Wait in the car with Eirwen.
REGINA	You are also under orders to drive Eirwen and me to the convention. So hurry up. I don't want her to catch cold. Her immune system is fragile.
SOLDIER	But…
REGINA	We can't risk her catching something. (*Looks at FRIEDA.*) Mmmm Interesting.
FRIEDA	Do I know you?
REGINA	I'm Dr Regina Woolf.
FRIEDA	Never heard of you.
REGINA	I'm a scientist. An important scientist.
FRIEDA	Mmmm. Interesting.
REGINA	Be quick, Eric. We cannot be late for this convention. Our future may depend on it.
FRIEDA	Then she went.
LITTLE OTTO	You can get down now, Mum. Well done.
BERTHA	Thank goodness for that.

	I'm not doing that again.
OTTO	Come on everyone back to business.
LITTLE OTTO	Dad, this show's struggling.
FRIEDA	**Scene Three. Little Otto tries to talk to his father.** Not for the first time.
LITTLE OTTO	Dad. About the show…
OTTO	Do your job.
LITTLE OTTO	It's about my job.
OTTO	Not now.
LITTLE OTTO	But I've got some ideas.
OTTO	Ideas don't put bums on seats.
SAM	(*There's a rumble of gunfire.*) Gunfire!
BERTHA	Those guns are getting a bit close.
OTTO	That's why I brought us here.
BERTHA	Yes, why was that? Everyone else is running away.
OTTO	Wars mean money.
FRIEDA	Then Eric the Soldier came back.
LITTLE OTTO	Dad.
OTTO	Too busy.
LITTLE OTTO	Eirwen, you then.
EIRWEN	I'd rather not.
LITTLE OTTO	I think you'll have to. There's nobody else.
EIRWEN	Will they understand?
FRIEDA	'Course they will. They're not as stupid as they look.
LITTLE OTTO	Can I just apologise for my sister?

EIRWEN	Alright. I'll do it! (*She climbs the ladder.*)
FRIEDA	So. The Soldier comes back and looks at Little Otto.
SOLDIER	Otto Frantz?
LITTLE OTTO	Um… Yes. Yes, I'm Otto Frantz.
FRIEDA	Little Otto is given a letter.
SOLDIER	Then this is for you. Young woman outside asked me to give it to you.
LITTLE OTTO	What is it?
SOLDIER	It's a letter. From Miss Lucretia Bolero.
LITTLE OTTO	Oh.
FRIEDA	He tries to give the letter back.
LITTLE OTTO	I'm not Otto Frantz.
SOLDIER	You said you were.
LITTLE OTTO	Yes, I know I said, but…
SOLDIER	So what is your name?
LITTLE OTTO	Otto Frantz, but…
SOLDIER	I'm here about your show. What time does it start?
LITTLE OTTO	You're a bit early.
SOLDIER	I'll wait. (*To FRIEDA.*) By the way what's the weather like down there?
LITTLE OTTO	Do you know if you'd said that to her yesterday you'd have won a prize.
SOLDIER	Would I?
LITTLE OTTO	Yeah. For the thousandth person to have said it. You'll forgive me if I don't laugh.

SOLDIER	Best get a seat near the front in case I can't see her.
LITTLE OTTO	You should be in showbiz, mate.
FRIEDA	The Soldier went. Little Otto tries to get rid of the letter again.
LITTLE OTTO	Sam? Help?
SAM	You are joking.
LITTLE OTTO	Please. Take the letter.
SAM	No way!
FRIEDA	Little Otto. Kneel quickly.
OTTO	Come on, come on. Chop. Chop. Otto you're not even in your costume yet.
LITTLE OTTO	(*Puts the letter away.*) Sorry, Dad.
SAM	Keep your hair on Shorty.
OTTO	You're sacked.
SAM	Of course I am.
BERTHA	Come on, Otto. Hurry up.
OTTO	Wait a minute. Little Otto?
FRIEDA	**Scene Four. In which we find out about Little Otto's secret, and his mother's part in it.**
BERTHA	No time for that.
OTTO	I haven't said what it is yet. Come over here.
FRIEDA	Mum and Little Otto tense. They know what is coming
LITTLE OTTO	Dad, about my ideas for the show.
OTTO	Ssh. Let me look at you. Are you growing? Bertha, is he growing?

BERTHA	Of course not.
OTTO	Stand up straight. Bertha, measure him.
BERTHA	Where's my tailor's chalk. Look, it's marked on the back of the set with the rest. You, Little Otto, me, Frieda. We're all short. *OTTO looks.* Now let's get on.
OTTO	Costumes everyone. Now where's Lucretia? *He goes.*
LITTLE OTTO	He's going to find out Mum. He is.
OTTO	Lucretia! Lucretia!
BERTHA	Not if I can help it.
LITTLE OTTO	I'm growing Mum.
BERTHA	Not so much.
LITTLE OTTO	I am. And he's going to find out.
BERTHA	I'll let your trousers down again, now get on.
OTTO	Come on everyone. Get your costume and props ready. Sort out your makeup. *They are all setting props, getting into costumes, and putting on make up.*
FRIEDA	This is where we live. Stage on top and dressing rooms underneath.

Scene Five. The Frantz family prepare to perform.

VERA	Frieda and Bertha are at their dressing tables. I am doing my nails.
FRIEDA	(*Looking at a mirror.*) Mirror, mirror on the wall. Who is the loveliest of all?

That's funny, it's not replying.
Sam! Sam!
My mirror's not working.
Mirror, mirror on the wall
(*As mirror.*) 'What the heck do you think you're looking at, shortarse?'
She puts on her beard.

VERA	Sam is looking at her. He obviously adores her. She notices him looking at her, but doesn't clock the love.
FRIEDA	What do you think Sam?
SAM	Gorgeous. Particularly the beard. It's a good look for you.
FRIEDA	I think I make it work.
SAM	You alright?
FRIEDA	Oh, yeah. Some day my Prince will come, eh?
SAM	When you least expect him.
FRIEDA	I'm just sick of being a dwarf.
SAM	Well, you never know. You might start growing.
FRIEDA	I'm not talking about my height, stupid. I'm talking about this play. I'm an actress. And I'm spending every night sticking on this smelly beard and falling over. When do I get to do Juliet, or Lady Macbeth?
SAM	Tonight you'll be Grumpy.
FRIEDA	You're not wrong there.
	BERTHA enters.
BERTHA	Frieda. Your costume. I've mended the rip. It should hold.
FRIEDA	Thanks Mum.

BERTHA	And here's Lucretia's,
FRIEDA	When she graces us with her presence. It's such a beautiful frock. What I wouldn't give…
SAM	Too lovely for Lucretia.
FRIEDA	She should be playing the witch.
	They laugh.
	It's true. I hate her.
BERTHA	(*Looking in the mirror.*) I'm getting too old for this.
OTTO	Don't be daft. You're a fine figure of a woman.
BERTHA	You think? You'd tell me if I wasn't. You'd be honest, Otto?
OTTO	Aren't I always?
BERTHA	Maybe we should just stop. This should be our last tour. I want grandchildren. How are Frieda and Otto ever going to meet anyone like this?
OTTO	This war could be great for us. People need cheering up. Nothing like the fear of imminent death to loosen the purse strings.
BERTHA	Just as long as the company get paid, Otto. I can't put them off again.
OTTO	We've weathered worse than this.
BERTHA	Have we? You look at the books.
OTTO	They'll always turn out to see us. Trust me. We're unique. They say they're coming to see Snow White, but we're the pull, the dwarfs. They'll always come to see the shortest man in the world, Otto Frantz.
BERTHA	Mmm, Yes, well…
OTTO	Bertha. There's something you're not saying.

BERTHA	No.
OTTO	Bertha, you now that I value honesty and truth above all things.
BERTHA	Well, I just heard that, Gustav's looking for work.
OTTO	What?!
BERTHA	I knew it.
OTTO	That charlatan! He has no standards. Appearing in stuff that peddles freaks and fakes. And that bearded lady? It's disgusting.
BERTHA	I'm wearing a beard.
OTTO	A fake one. It's different.
BERTHA	Gustav is short, out of work and we need more dwarfs for the show.
OTTO	Gustav Drool will be in my show over my dead body. Sam, call the full company. Time for one of my pep talks.
SAM	Oh I'm really looking forward to that.
OTTO	Bertha. Gustav.
BERTHA	What about him?
OTTO	Is he shorter than me? Is he?
BERTHA	Time for that pep talk I think.
	She goes.
SAM	Alright, gather round everyone. Mr Frantz wants to speak.
OTTO	Right.
FRIEDA	**Scene Six. Otto Frantz delivers one of his famous and inspiring pep talks.**
SAM	There's that gunfire again.

BERTHA	Not more guns?
OTTO	Thunder. Good for business. A bit of rain. The punters will need somewhere to shelter. So. How long have we been touring this show?
SAM	Too long.
OTTO	A long time. And I know things have been tough lately. But this place is going to be good for us. I can feel it, in my bones. How many are in?
LITTLE OTTO	Thirteen tickets sold.
BERTHA	Bad luck. Thirteen.
OTTO	Don't talk soft. We make our own luck. Somebody, sit out front to make up the numbers.
LITTLE OTTO	There's nobody spare.
BERTHA	Then throw somebody out. One of the kids.
SAM	Will we get paid, this week? Just asking.
OTTO	So, let the laughs lift the roof. And Lucretia… Lucretia? Where is she?
LITTLE OTTO	Oh, Dad. This is for you.
OTTO	What's that?
LITTLE OTTO	A letter
OTTO	Read it. I haven't got my specs.
LITTLE OTTO	Frieda.

He gives it to FRIEDA.

28

FRIEDA	If I must… It's from Lucretia. 'Dear Otto I know this will come as a surprise I know you won't like it. But I'm leaving. In fact by the time you read this I'll be far away. And I'm taking Roger with me.'
OTTO	Roger!
FRIEDA	Roger.
BERTHA	The Prince!
LITTLE OTTO	I hadn't even noticed he was missing.
SAM	Always was a waste of space.
FRIEDA	'Roger has been called up to join the army. He and I are getting married.'
BERTHA	Aw!
OTTO	Aw? He's the Prince. Our show!
FRIEDA	'Frankly, I've been wanting to leave for a long time. Your show…'
	She dribbles away.
SAM	What? Your show what?
FRIEDA	Nothing.
OTTO	Read it.
FRIEDA	Alright, but don't blame me. 'Your show is rubbish. It's old fashioned. It's not funny. It's going nowhere. I've got a bad back from bending over to talk to you, which wouldn't be so bad if you ever listened. Frankly, I'd rather be cleaning toilets.'
OTTO	She'd rather be cleaning toilets?!

	Than working with me?!
FRIEDA	Don't shoot me. I'm just the messenger.
OTTO	Cleaning toilets? She said that?
FRIEDA	(*Looks at the letter.*) 'Cleaning toilets. With my bare hands.'
OTTO	Cleaning toilets?! I've treated her like my own daughter.
FRIEDA	Maybe that was the problem.
OTTO	How could she do this to me? How could she? After all I've…
LITTLE OTTO	Dad goes ballistic.
BERTHA	We'll have to cancel.
OTTO	No.
BERTHA	Sam, nip out front and give them their money back.
OTTO	No! No! No! The show must go on. Line up.
FRIEDA	**Scene Seven. Otto tries to make the best of a bad job.**
BERTHA	This is ridiculous.
OTTO	Line up. What have we got?
SAM	Four dwarfs, no Snow White, no Prince. Queen's a puppet.
OTTO	Kneel down, Sam. You can be a dwarf.
BERTHA	Otto! No fakes.

OTTO	Alright then. You can do the Prince.
SAM	Me?
OTTO	Yes.
SAM	Well, I suppose...
FRIEDA	He's too old.
SAM	Am I?
FRIEDA	'Course you are.
SAM	Yeah. Yeah, you're right. I'm too old. Anyway, I'm the huntsman.
OTTO	You can double. They're never on at the same time.
SAM	Oh no, I can't.
OTTO	It's not a big part. You'll have to.
SAM	I'd rather be Snow White.
OTTO	Snow White? We've no Snow White.
FRIEDA	I thought, This is it. My moment. Scene whatever... Frieda gets her big chance. I stepped forward.
OTTO	What Frieda? I'm thinking.
FRIEDA	Me! There's me.
OTTO	You?
FRIEDA	Dad, Give me a chance.
OTTO	No.

31

Nobody'd believe it.

FRIEDA   It's a fairy tale, for goodness sake.
Once upon a time in a beautiful land.
They don't have to believe it.

OTTO   It may be a fairy tale.
It still needs to be truthful.

BERTHA   Otto, give the girl a chance.

OTTO   No.

LITTLE OTTO   Dad.

OTTO   No.

FRIEDA   Please.

BERTHA   Otto, please.

LITTLE OTTO   Dad, Give her a chance.

OTTO   Not now.
She hasn't even got black hair.

FRIEDA   Neither had Lucretia.
I'll wear her wig.

BERTHA   She deserves the same chance as any one else.
Anyway, what choice have you got?

OTTO   Alright.
Get the frock on.

FRIEDA   Yes.

OTTO   But this is a one off.

FRIEDA   Will it fit?

BERTHA   I'll make it.

OTTO   And a rousing chorus of the family song to
warm us up.

Everyone races to get everything ready.

FAMILY SONG

There's a great many things
In this big wide world
For which I'd give you thanks
(Big thanks)
A wave from a boy
A smile from a girl
Or a key to open banks
(Fat chance)

CHORUS

But there's just one thing
You can kindly stuff
And that's what I'll now name
I'm not being funny
You can keep your money
We'll never be all the same
We'll never never never never
Ever ever ever ever
Never be all the same.
(Again)
We'll never never never never
Ever ever ever ever
Never be all the same.
I'm not you
And you're not me
This isn't rocket science.
(No fear)
Some are short
And some are fat
And some are even giants.
(Not here)
I'm not being funny
You can keep your money
We'll never be all the same

REPEAT CHORUS.

OTTO   **Scene Eight. The Frantz family present
their celebrated...**

FRIEDA	…and past its best…
OTTO	**…celebrated version of Snow White and the Seven Dwarfs.** Sam, set the stage. Vera do the costume check.
VERA	Bertha, Queen cardboard cut-out. Check. Three Dwarf costumes. Check. Sam. Huntsman's cloak. Check. Prince's crown. Check. Frieda, Wig and Snow White dress. Check. Me, top hat and tails. Check it out.
BERTHA	Once upon a time, in the middle of winter, snowflakes were falling like feathers from the sky. At a castle window framed in ebony sat a young queen sewing. As she was stitching, she pricked her finger, and three drops of blood fell down upon the snow. Because the red colour looked so beautiful there on the snow she thought to herself: 'Would that I had a child as white as snow, lips as rosy red as blood, and with hair as ebony black as the window frame!' Soon afterwards a baby girl was born to her – as white as snow, lips as red as blood, and with hair as black as ebony, and she was called Snow White. At the birth of the child, the Queen died.

In the middle of the speech EIRWEN makes her entrance. She sees OTTO.

EIRWEN	And that's when I, Eirwen, came in. I'd been waiting for Regina and Eric in the car and I got bored. I saw Otto. I'd never seen anything like him. What are you?
OTTO	The boss. What are you?

EIRWEN	Are you real?
SAM	You're in the wrong place love. Seats round the front. The front. This is the backstage.
OTTO	What's wrong with her? Is she daft?
EIRWEN	What's that? It's lovely.
SAM	She's going on stage!
OTTO	Somebody grab her!
SAM	This way, Dear.
EIRWEN	What are you doing? Take your hands off me.
OTTO	Somebody get rid of her.
SAM	Little Otto do the sound effects.
BERTHA	Mirror, Mirror on the wall Who is the fairest of them all? *Nothing happens.* AGAIN Mirror, Mirror on the wall Who is the fairest of them all? *Clearly making this up to buy time.* Tell me please, so I can see Is it you or is it me?
OTTO	The mirror. The mirror. Who does the mirror?
SAM	Roger.
BERTHA	How much longer must I wait? Till someone notices my state?
LITTLE OTTO	I'll do it. (*Shouts.*) You are!
BERTHA	Too late.
LITTLE OTTO	Sorry, I forgot.

35

BERTHA	Never in all my career…
OTTO	No time for that now.
SAM	(*To FRIEDA.*) Good luck.
BERTHA	But the day came when the Queen asked the mirror, and the mirror gave a different answer.
	On stage again.
	Mirror, Mirror on the wall Who is the fairest of them all?
LITTLE OTTO	Queen, you are of beauty rare But Snow White with her ebony hair Is a thousand thousand times more fair.
BERTHA	Snow White! Snow White!
FRIEDA	That was when Eirwen walked onto the stage
EIRWEN	Hello little person.
BERTHA	What?
EIRWEN	Are you real?
BERTHA	Who the heck are you?
FRIEDA	But Sam saved the day.
	SAM runs on stage.
BERTHA	Ah, huntsman! Do something.
SAM	(*As huntsman.*) Just one of the servant girls wandered up from the scullery, your majesty. Off you go love. Now.
EIRWEN	Where have the little people gone? I want to see them again?
SAM	In a minute. (*Lifts her off.*) Go on. I'll be back.
BERTHA	Huntsman, take Snow White into the wood

	To the deepest darkest part There you must slit her throat And bring me back her heart.
SAM	Your majesty.
EIRWEN	(*Has wandered back.*) You are real. I thought you were just in stories. You're so sweet.
BERTHA	Look love, will you just push off We're trying to do a job up here.
LITTLE OTTO	You get off that stage.
OTTO	Give me strength. Get to the cottage. Quickly. Get to the cottage in the woods.
FRIEDA	And skip my bit? No way. Come on Sam.

SAM and FRIEDA run on.

	Oh, huntsman we are so far away from home. Shouldn't we be getting back?
SAM	This is as far as we go Snow White.

He takes out a knife.

FRIEDA	Huntsman, why the knife? And you look so strange.
OTTO	Come on get on with it. Faster!
SAM	(*At a very fast pace.*) Oh, it's no good I can't do it?
FRIEDA	Do what?
SAM	Kill you.
FRIEDA	Kill me?
SAM	Kill you.
FRIEDA	Kill me?

SAM   Kill you and cut out your heart.

FRIEDA   But why?

SAM   The Queen.

FRIEDA   The Queen?

SAM   The Queen.

FRIEDA   The Queen.

SAM   Yes. The Queen ordered me to kill you.

OTTO   Jump to the dwarfs.
The dwarfs.
That's what they come for.
It's the best bit.
(*To audience.*) So Snow White comes to a little
cottage in the woods.

FRIEDA   Oh look.
A little cottage in the woods.

OTTO   Come on.

*They order into a line, bumping into each other and
falling over while doing it.*

What's been going on here?

Turns to the next in line.

BERTHA   Yeah, what's been going on here?

Turns to the next in line.

LITTLE OTTO   Yeah, what's been going on here?

Turns to the next in line. There's no one there.

The other four must still be digging.

LITTLE OTTO sneezes.

BERTHA   Oh Sneezy.
Wipe your nose.

LITTLE OTTO wipes it on his sleeve.

BERTHA	Not on your sleeve. No, Not on my sleeve.
OTTO	Wait a minute. Look at the bed.
BERTHA	What is it now, Grumpy?
OTTO	There's something in your bed, Snotty.
LITTLE OTTO	What is it? What is it? You look.
BERTHA	It's just a girl.
LITTLE OTTO	A girl, in my bed?
FRIEDA	That'll be the day. **Scene Nine. The strangers come back, and we find out what they came for.** The soldier.
EIRWEN	Pass me the jacket. I'll be Eric.
FRIEDA	And Regina. We all looked at Sam.
SAM	No.
FRIEDA	Sam!
LITTLE OTTO	Wear the wig and the glasses.
SAM	I'm the stage manager.
FRIEDA	Sam!
SAM	I'm a man!
LITTLE OTTO	Sam! You are playing Regina. Get on with it.
SAM	Alright. Alright.
LITTLE OTTO	Right, Soldier, you start the scene and Regina you come in later. I'll give you your cue.
SOLDIER	I am an officer in the state defence force.
OTTO	What's going on now? Get off my stage.

SOLDIER	We have taken over the administration of this district. This show is closed down.
BERTHA	What?
SOLDIER	This takes effect immediately.
OTTO	I think there must have been a misunderstanding.
SOLDIER	I don't know what's going on down there, but up here in the world there's a war on. The country is being cleansed of its riff raff. Lines are being drawn. Borders closed.
OTTO	No, no, no. Borders don't apply to us. Never have.
SOLDIER	They do now. People are being returned to their place of origin.
OTTO	We don't have one.
SOLDIER	Then go back to fairyland. In such times as these we must be careful. All shows must be referred for approval.
OTTO	Then we'll do it.
SOLDIER	This show would not receive approval. It is a freak show.
OTTO	It's a family show.
BERTHA	A fairy tale.
SOLDIER	In no way is this suitable for a family audience. The authorities no longer allow the public display of the disabled. It encourages laughter.
OTTO	Laughter is surely a good thing!
SOLDIER	We do not encourage laughing at the afflicted. It is not a laughing matter. It is offensive and humiliating.

OTTO	Bertha, are you offended?
BERTHA	No.
OTTO	Are you humiliated?
BERTHA	Sometimes. By you.
SOLDIER	You will close down this show immediately.
OTTO	No. You can't do this This is our livelihood.
SOLDIER	I'll be back in the morning to give you instructions. It is no longer safe around here. And if I were you young lady, I would take off that beard. It doesn't suit you.
LITTLE OTTO	That was when Regina came in
REGINA	(*Enters.*) Eric. It's Eirwen. She's gone missing.
SOLDIER	I'm just coming.
REGINA	Hurry. She's not in the car. *She leaves.*
FRIEDA	Well done Sam.
SAM	Your face!
BERTHA	Where will we go?
SOLDIER	A transit camp.
FRIEDA	Can I ask something?
SOLDIER	Yes.
FRIEDA	What's the weather like up there? *SOLDIER leaves.*

Scene Ten. Otto makes a decision.

OTTO	(*Finally calms down.*) Sam. Has he gone?
SAM	Yes.

OTTO	Right, then come on. We're off. Pack the stuff.
BERTHA	Where?
OTTO	If they don't want us round here, we'll find somewhere that does. Which way did he go?
LITTLE OTTO	That way. Left.
OTTO	Then we're going this way. Right!
LITTLE OTTO	Alright then. Places for moving everybody. Sam, get the costumes.

There's a lot of activity. SAM is throwing costumes into a trunk when EIRWEN pops up. She signs to him to be quiet.

SAM	**Scene Eleven. Sam makes a discovery.** What are you doing there?
EIRWEN	Please don't tell on me.
SAM	Get out, there is something weird about you.
EIRWEN	They'll take me back to that place. I can't go back. I can't. Please.
SAM	All right. But be quiet. Hide under the dressing table.
FRIEDA	So, That night, under cover of darkness. We took all our stuff and left town.

FAMILY SONG

(Humming)
There's a great many things
In this big wide world
For which I'd give you thanks
(Big thanks)
A wave from a boy
A smile from a girl

Or a key to open banks
(Fat chance)

CHORUS
But there's just one thing
You can kindly stuff
And that's what I'll now name

SUNG
I'm not being funny
You can keep your money
We'll never never never never
Ever ever ever ever
Never be all the same.
(Again)
We'll never never never never
Ever ever ever ever
Never be all the same.

FRIEDA   **Scene Twelve. On the run.**
So, somehow we've come to somewhere else.
It looks pretty much like everywhere else.
We're always moving. When people talk about
home they usually mean a place. To me home
is these people. Sometimes I wish there was a
place I could be where I was so familiar I was
virtually invisible. But we're never invisible.
Ever, anywhere. There is no place in the world,
no street we can walk down where we are not
stared at, where we're not a theatrical event.
Wherever we go we're a show.
Some people want to be a somebody.
I just want to be a nobody.
And a great actress.

OTTO   Freak show. Freak show?! Who does she think
she is? This is a family show. They come
because we tell a good story. Gustav. Now he
likes freak shows. Close him down.

LITTLE OTTO   Who's Gustav?

OTTO	(*OTTO doesn't answer.*) I'm going to help Sam.
FRIEDA	Who's Gustav?
BERTHA	Oh, he's just somebody your father and I used to know. We worked with him. Before we were married.
FRIEDA	And…
BERTHA	Nothing.
FRIEDA	Mum. You went out with him.
LITTLE OTTO	Did you go out with him?
BERTHA	No. Well, maybe once or twice. Long time ago. Before the war.
FRIEDA	What happened?
BERTHA	Dancing. Just a couple of times.
FRIEDA	And was he short?
BERTHA	Yes.
FRIEDA	Very short?
BERTHA	Yes.
LITTLE OTTO	Shorter than Dad?!
BERTHA	Sssh. Otto never liked him.
OTTO	(*Enters.*) What?
FRIEDA	Nothing.
LITTLE OTTO	Nothing.
FRIEDA	**Scene Thirteen.**
LITTLE OTTO	Shouldn't have a scene thirteen.
FRIEDA	Why not?
LITTLE OTTO	Unlucky.
FRIEDA	Well this one is.
LITTLE OTTO	Who for?

FRIEDA	You. On your knees. Quick. **Scene Thirteen. Little Otto's little secret. Again. And how it all went pear-shaped.**
OTTO	Little Otto.
LITTLE OTTO	What, Dad?
OTTO	How tall are you?
LITTLE OTTO	Well.
BERTHA	Let me measure him. Sam, give me the tape.
	SAM does so.
	There see. No change. You, Little Otto, me and Frieda. All short. I've just got to…
	Goes to the costumes then leaps back.
	There's somebody in the costumes.
FRIEDA	Sam!
SAM	It's alright. You can come out.
	EIRWEN reveals herself.
FRIEDA	Eirwen crawls out from under the dressing table.
EIRWEN	Hallo.
FRIEDA	What are you doing here?
EIRWEN	Don't take me back. Please don't take me back.
FRIEDA	You can't stay here.
LITTLE OTTO	Why not?
FRIEDA	We don't need more trouble.
BERTHA	Let the poor girl breathe.
LITTLE OTTO	Where are you from?

EIRWEN	The Institute. They call it the Institute.
LITTLE OTTO	Is it a prison?
EIRWEN	A prison? I don't know.
LITTLE OTTO	Are there bars on the windows?
EIRWEN	Yes. Bars. And guards. Don't send me back. I hate it there.
FRIEDA	What about your parents?
EIRWEN	Parents?
FRIEDA	Mother and father?
EIRWEN	Don't understand.
OTTO	Everyone has parents.
EIRWEN	Not me.
OTTO	You see, the daddy gets together with the mummy and...well...and...they...the daddy... and the mummy...Bertha, you tell her.
BERTHA	Forgotten where babies come from, Otto? Parents are the people who made you.
EIRWEN	Regina. Regina made me.
FRIEDA	Her? She's horrible.
BERTHA	So she's your mum.
EIRWEN	Is she?
FRIEDA	What are your earliest memories?
EIRWEN	My first memory? My first memory is...white.
FRIEDA	White?
EIRWEN	The colour white. Is white a colour? White light. White as snow. No. Whiter than snow. Snow is sometimes grey.
LITTLE OTTO	There must be people there.

EIRWEN	Don't make me go back. Please don't. I could help. Surely there's something I could do.
OTTO	Company meeting. You stay over here.
FRIEDA	(*To audience.*) We had a family conference. And
OTTO	Meet our new Snow White.
FRIEDA	What?
OTTO	Look at her. She's perfect.
FRIEDA	No.
OTTO	Little Otto, give her a script.
FRIEDA	But you don't even know if she can act.
OTTO	No, but she looks right and that's half the battle. She'll soon pick it up. It's not rocket science. You can teach her.
FRIEDA	No.
BERTHA	Frieda,
FRIEDA	No. That's my part.
SAM	I thought she did it beautifully.
OTTO	Our show is not a beautiful show. It's a funny show. We make people laugh That's what we do. And you will never be Snow White.
FRIEDA	Why not?
OTTO	You are a dwarf A dwarf.
FRIEDA	Dad, it's only pretend. I'm an actress, I'm not really a dwarf.

	Dwarfs live in little cottages in the forest and dig in the mines. In case you haven't noticed we don't.
OTTO	Don't you get clever with me young lady. As far as the punters are concerned you are a dwarf. You are not Will never be Snow White.
FRIEDA	Why not?
OTTO	Because people will laugh.
FRIEDA	They won't.
OTTO	They've been laughing at us for thousands of years. They're not going to stop now.
FRIEDA	They don't.
OTTO	Frieda. You walk down the street they laugh. At least in here we take their money for doing it.
FRIEDA	Why can't I be Snow White?
OTTO	It just isn't going to happen. Not in my show.
FRIEDA	Then maybe I'll leave.
OTTO	Go on then.
FRIEDA	I will.
OTTO	Do. I'm sure you'll do very well in the big wide world.
BERTHA	Gustav would take her on.
OTTO	(*Now very angry.*) I'm sure he would. He'd put you in a Snow White dress alright, and then fire you out of a cannon into a big bowl of rice pudding, because that's what

dwarfs do. You'll be a freak. Is that what you want?

FRIEDA No Dad. I just want a chance.

OTTO This is the best chance you'll get. I suggest you take it. Right. I am now going into town with Sam to rustle up business for Snow White and the Seven Dwarfs, a family show.

FRIEDA Dad.

OTTO Don't you gainsay me girl.
I have a good feeling about this place.
Welcome to the show, love.
Little Otto, teach the new girl the moves.

OTTO leaves.

FRIEDA Mum.

BERTHA Frieda, If you're expecting me to take your side against your dad, you're wrong. He's trying to hold this together. There's a war on. We're on the run. We don't know where the next meal is coming from, and we're doing Snow White and we're already three dwarfs down. Let's measure this young girl for the frock.

VERA Oh get over yourself.

FRIEDA **Scene fourteen. The rehearsal.**

EIRWEN (*To FRIEDA.*) I've read about you in stories. Why are you so short?

FRIEDA Pardon?

EIRWEN You are short. Why?

LITTLE OTTO Can we get on?

EIRWEN Are you magic?

FRIEDA We're short because our parents are short.

EIRWEN You're not short.

LITTLE OTTO Yes, I am.

EIRWEN No, you are not.

LITTLE OTTO Let's rehearse?

FRIEDA (*To EIRWEN.*) You'll need the script.

EIRWEN No. I know it.

FRIEDA Of course you do.

EIRWEN We'll see.

LITTLE OTTO I am Prince Charming handsome and brave.
My father wishes me to marry a Princess from
a neighbouring Country,

EIRWEN That is wrong.

LITTLE OTTO What?

EIRWEN It is wrong.

LITTLE OTTO It's not.

EIRWEN It is.

LITTLE OTTO It isn't.

EIRWEN Page ten.

FRIEDA picks up the script. Looks.

Line fifteen.

They all look.

Word three.
Wants. My father wants me to marry a Princess
from a neighbouring country…

FRIEDA She's right. How?

LITTLE OTTO That's weird.

EIRWEN I read it.

FRIEDA And remembered it.

EIRWEN Yes.

LITTLE OTTO	All of it?
EIRWEN	Of course. And I have a question about the next bit.
FRIEDA	Right, now I'm scared.
EIRWEN	I want to be in Love. So I have come here to the forest to search my heart. What does that mean?
LITTLE OTTO	You know about love. Everyone knows about love. It's what makes the world go round.
FRIEDA	And makes babies.
EIRWEN	I don't think that's right.
FRIEDA	Can we get on with this?
EIRWEN	Prince. Entering. I am Prince Charming handsome and brave. (*To LITTLE OTTO.*) Show me where I move.
	LITTLE OTTO steers her through the next bit. LITTLE OTTO is smitten. FRIEDA stunned.
	Prince. My father wants me to marry a Princess from a neighbouring country; I want to be in Love. So I have come here to the forest to search my heart. Snow White. Entering. My stepmother has sent me to find wood for the fire. The Prince hides behind a bush. Prince. Who is that? It's a girl. I'll hide here.
	She stops.
	Is something wrong?
FRIEDA	Yes.
LITTLE OTTO	No.
FRIEDA	Yes.
LITTLE OTTO	Well she's a quick learner.
FRIEDA	She's a robot.

LITTLE OTTO	Perhaps we should try again.
EIRWEN	Very well.
LITTLE OTTO	This time just say the parts marked Snow White.
FRIEDA	With feelings.
EIRWEN	Feelings?
FRIEDA	Like a human being.
LITTLE OTTO	She's a girl, on her own in the woods. She meets a handsome young man. He sees her and falls in love.
EIRWEN	And make babies?
LITTLE OTTO	She's a fast worker.
FRIEDA	So we went on with the rehearsal. And by the time Otto got back.
OTTO	No luck. We'll have to keep moving. They wouldn't even let us put up our posters. There's a ban.
SAM	We did find this though, a missing girl poster of Eirwen. All over the place. She's not just a nobody.
FRIEDA	So we'll have to send her back.
EIRWEN	No.
OTTO	Yes. We're in deep enough trouble as it is.
LITTLE OTTO	Wait a minute, Dad. Watch this. Play the scene.
EIRWEN	My stepmother has sent me to find wood for the fire.
LITTLE OTTO	Who is that? It's a girl. I'll hide here.
EIRWEN	I have never wandered so far into the forest before. The animals and birds are my friends. I am safe here.

LITTLE OTTO	Who is she? Who is that beautiful girl?
EIRWEN	I never get time to myself since my mother died.
	LITTLE OTTO jumps out.
	Oh, you startled me. Who are you?
LITTLE OTTO	Oh just a servant. Who are you?
EIRWEN	Snow White.
LITTLE OTTO	Are you a Princess?
EIRWEN	No. I'm just an ordinary person. There's nothing special about me.
LITTLE OTTO	On the contrary. You are special, very special.
FRIEDA	They kiss, for a little longer than strictly necessary. All right. Break it up.
EIRWEN	(*To OTTO.*) Is that alright?
OTTO	Alright? Alright? You are perfect. Where's that poster.
	He takes the wanted poster and tears it up.
	You are going nowhere. We've got a show.
FRIEDA	But Dad.
OTTO	If it's more bad news I don't want to hear it.
FRIEDA	It's about her.
OTTO	Jealousy, Frieda, is not an attractive quality. She's perfect.
FRIEDA	Too perfect. There's something strange about her.
OTTO	Don't. Don't. Don't.
EIRWEN	Excuse me… Why is little Otto so tall?

FRIEDA	**Scene Fifteen. The Poo hits the fan. Little Otto's little secret comes out.**
OTTO	What?
LITTLE OTTO	No.
EIRWEN	He says he's short but he is taller than me.
OTTO	Little Otto. Let me look at you.
	He stands near him.
	Bertha. Give me your tape measure.
BERTHA	I don't know where it is.
OTTO	Round your neck.
LITTLE OTTO	Dad, we should be getting on.
OTTO	Shut up.
	Measures him. He can't reach.
	Sam.
	(*To BERTHA.*) How long have you known?
LITTLE OTTO	Dad.
	OTTO ignores him.
BERTHA	Years.
OTTO	Years? Years?!
BERTHA	Yes.
OTTO	All this time and you've been keeping it from me.
BERTHA	Well, you've got eyes too.
OTTO	I trusted you to tell me the truth.
BERTHA	Otto, nobody can tell you anything.
OTTO	Out.
LITTLE OTTO	What?!

OTTO	You're out of the show.
BERTHA	Otto, No.
LITTLE OTTO	Dad!
OTTO	We can't have a tall dwarf. We'd be laughing stocks.
LITTLE OTTO	Dad, please.
OTTO	What did I do?
LITTLE OTTO	What did I do?
BERTHA	You just grew, love.
LITTLE OTTO	Dad, I'm still your son.
OTTO	I can't look even look at you.
LITTLE OTTO	Dad, I'm still me.
OTTO	Yes, but what's that? We're the Frantz family. We're dwarfs. We're short. We are different. And look at you. What are you? Normal. Average. Boring.
LITTLE OTTO	I'm still your son.
OTTO	You lot get ready to move. I've got to see if I can rustle up a few more dwarfs.
BERTHA	Otto.
OTTO	I'm not talking to you.
LITTLE OTTO	Sam, help me pack. Please.
SAM	Are you alright?
LITTLE OTTO	Yes.
SAM	Looks like it.
LITTLE OTTO	I had great plans for this show. I could make it much better.
SAM	Then tell him.

LITTLE OTTO	He won't listen.
SAM	Well, make him. You should shout a bit. You'll feel better.
LITTLE OTTO	I've never been much of a shouter.
SAM	Me neither. You need to stand up for yourself. Otto takes up too much space.
LITTLE OTTO	He's the smallest man in the world.
SAM	He's a big bully. Come on. Stand up for yourself. Be big.
LITTLE OTTO	I don't want to be big. I want to be like the rest of my family. I know when I'm not wanted. Bye Sam.
VERA	You going to tell them he's gone?
SAM	No, and neither are you.
	OTTO and BERTHA are packing up. Not speaking.
OTTO	I trusted you.
BERTHA	Put a sock in it, Otto. I was looking after him. Size doesn't matter, Otto.
OTTO	How can you say that? How can you say that? All our life is about our size.
BERTHA	No it's not. The things that make us like each other are more important than the things that make us different.
OTTO	Am I going mad?
BERTHA	It's a little difference.
OTTO	It's a gigantic difference.
BERTHA	I wouldn't love him more if he was smaller. Right. Everybody ready?
	They all gather. LITTLE OTTO is missing.

FRIEDA	Where's Little Otto?
VERA	Gone
OTTO	Gone?
SAM	Vera?!
VERA	They had to know.
BERTHA	You were too hard on him.
OTTO	I've got to be hard on him. He hasn't got our advantages. He can't just stand there while people look at him. He's going to actually have to do something. Now come on.
FRIEDA	So we moved on. Little Otto? This is your bit. None of us were there.
VERA	I was.
EIRWEN	Don't tell them what happens.
VERA	Why not?
EIRWEN	You'll spoil the story.
LITTLE OTTO	**Scene Sixteen. What happened next.**
	REGINA and SOLDIER enter.
REGINA	Where are they?
SOLDIER	They were here. I swear they were here.
REGINA	And Eirwen was with them?
SOLDIER	So the villagers said.
REGINA	Well, they're not here now, are they?
SOLDIER	Sorry, Regina.
REGINA	We need her back. My research. The consequences if she's discovered…
SOLDIER	We'll find her.

57

REGINA	You'd better. This stupid war, and this stupid, stupid government. Telling me what I can and cannot do.
SOLDIER	Regina!
REGINA	You have to work for them, Eric. It doesn't mean you have to believe all their nonsense. I am a scientist. You know how important this is. I have worked all my life for this. They are stuck in the past. We're talking about the future. And Eirwen is that future.
SOLDIER	I'll have the area scoured. They can't get far. (*Sees LITTLE OTTO.*) Him. He's one of them.
REGINA	You. Boy.
LITTLE OTTO	Yes?
REGINA	Are you Otto Frantz?
LITTLE OTTO	Yes. Yes, I am.
REGINA	You're just the man I need.
VERA	Little Otto. Don't go.
REGINA	There's big world waiting for you, young man.
LITTLE OTTO	(*To VERA.*) Ssssh. (*To REGINA.*) What did you have in mind?
FRIEDA	That's the end of part one.
OTTO	Go and buy sweets, good for business.
BERTHA	Otto, no! It rots their teeth.
OTTO	Oh yeah it does that. Good for dentists. I should have been a dentist. Have you ever seen a poor dentist?
FRIEDA	You still here? Go.

Part Two

FRIEDA	So once upon a time Part Two. We were on the run again. We moved from town to town. Every night we do the show in a different place. Then after dark we pack up and we run. **Scene One. A shortage of dwarfs.** Found Little Otto?
OTTO	I've been looking for dwarfs. Real dwarfs. I telephoned everybody I know. Most of the shows have been shut down.
BERTHA	Phone Gustav. Gustav's a dwarf, and he's a good actor. Phone him.
OTTO	I already have.
BERTHA	And?
OTTO	He's not there, and nobody knows where he's gone.
FRIEDA	We heard a car pull up. **Scene Two. Trouble.**
OTTO	Eirwen hide.
VERA	Don't come out.
FRIEDA	It was Dr Regina Woolf. *SAM as REGINA.*
REGINA	Well, well, well. We meet again.
OTTO	Fancy that?
REGINA	You took some finding.
FRIEDA	You just needed to look under a toadstool.

REGINA	I was just wondering if you had seen a young girl?
FRIEDA	Me?
REGINA	Witty as ever, I see. She was with me the last time we met. Very pretty. We haven't seen her since.
BERTHA	No, we haven't seen her.
REGINA	I just thought you might.
OTTO	Well, we haven't. Can we start?
REGINA	Not performing, I hope?
OTTO	No, rehearsing. Performing is banned.
REGINA	Mind if I watch?
OTTO	Be my guest. So the Queen went to her mirror.
BERTHA	(*Reading Queen.*) Mirror, mirror on the wall I am the loveliest of all I never ever will grow old But I need jewels and I need gold Those dwarfs are the ones I need To slake my thirst and fill my greed. Otto this isn't very good.
	OTTO gives her a look.
REGINA	Well, I for one am loving it.
BERTHA	Oh alright. Their jewels are what I want to see. Get those dwarfs bring them to me.
OTTO	OK. So there's a big flash. Sam's got that sorted. And Ta Dah!

REGINA	What are they?
OTTO	Four cut-out dwarfs. Sam made them.
REGINA	Amazing. Two-dimensional. You can hardly tell them from the real thing.
	Claps.
	Well that was lovely. Shame no audience will ever see it. And someone seems to be missing. Snow White. Now where is she?
OTTO	What do you want?
REGINA	I believe you have something that belongs to me.
OTTO	Madam, everything we possess is our own. Bought and paid for.
REGINA	Is that so? We'll see. Come in.
	LITTLE OTTO enters.
BERTHA	Little Otto, my baby. What are you doing with her?
LITTLE OTTO	Mum.
REGINA	Enough of the fond reunion. Little Otto, find Eirwen.
LITTLE OTTO	Here she is hiding behind the cut-out dwarfs.
BERTHA	Otto!
FRIEDA	Eirwen pauses for a moment, looks at us and then falls into Regina's arms.
REGINA	Darling, you're safe. Thank goodness.
EIRWEN	Oh it's been terrible. Terrible.
REGINA	There, there. Are you alright?
EIRWEN	They made me work, sweep and tidy and make beds.

61

BERTHA	What?!
FRIEDA	Only in the play! Not really.
REGINA	Poor dear girl. You're safe now.
LITTLE OTTO	Let's get you away from this place.
BERTHA	No, you're staying. Little Otto, you belong with us.
LITTLE OTTO	I'm not so little Mum. And I don't belong. Come on Eirwen.

LITTLE OTTO and EIRWEN leave.

BERTHA	Now wait a minute.
LITTLE OTTO	Right, on with the story. Eirwen, play Eric the soldier.
SOLDIER	This show is closing. Now.
BERTHA	You again!
SOLDIER	You're in deep trouble now.
REGINA	Kidnapping is a serious offence.
BERTHA	We did not kidnap that girl. We helped her.
SOLDIER	Don't make it worse. There is a war on. The show is banned. All these things are confiscated. Pack a single bag and line up.
OTTO	Don't you touch any of it. We will leave under our own steam.
BERTHA	What will happen to everything?
SOLDIER	You won't need it where you're going.
OTTO	You will not lay a finger on it. We'll starve.
REGINA	You should have thought of that when you took my daughter.

OTTO	Your daughter! She said she had no mother.
REGINA	Well, she does. Me.
BERTHA	We helped her.
REGINA	Don't be ridiculous.
BERTHA	You've seen her. Is there anything wrong with her?
REGINA	She looks well enough.
BERTHA	She eats well enough too.
REGINA	Take them away.
SOLDIER	Right. Get ready to go.
OTTO	No. Wait. You're a scientist, right?
REGINA	Yes.
OTTO	Can I have a word with you?
REGINA	What could you possibly have to say to me?
OTTO	In private please.
REGINA	Then make it quick.
	They step aside.
FRIEDA	**Scene Three. Otto does a deal.**
SAM	(*To FRIEDA.*) Are you alright?
FRIEDA	Yes. It couldn't last, Sam. You can't have Snow White without dwarfs. Where will you go?
SAM	I'm going nowhere. While there's still a show.
FRIEDA	You might have to Sam. There's nothing here for you.
SAM	Yes there is.
FRIEDA	What?
SAM	Well…

SOLDIER   Eh, you. What you doing here? With them?

SAM   What do you mean?

SOLDIER   Well, you're not one of them, are you?

SAM   No.

SOLDIER   Then why are you with them? You don't have
            to be with them.

SAM   They're my friends. I like them.

SOLDIER   Takes all sorts, I guess.

OTTO   (*Returns.*) Come on everybody. Get the stuff.
            We're off.

BERTHA   Where?

OTTO   We're going to this Institute.

FRIEDA   Hang on. Why?

OTTO   We're putting on a show.

FRIEDA   What?

OTTO   I've done a deal. Come on.

FRIEDA   I'm not going with her.

OTTO   We get to work. Little Otto will be there. It's
            that or prison. We disappear, like every other
            dwarf has.

BERTHA   Who's the audience?

OTTO   Scientists.

BERTHA   Really? Do they have a sense of humour?

SOLDIER   Regina.

REGINA   Yes, Eric.

SOLDIER   You can't do this.

REGINA   I can do what I like.

SOLDIER   You know the state policy on people like these.

REGINA Yes.

SOLDIER They are officially waste.

REGINA Then they won't be missed.

SOLDIER I have to follow orders.

REGINA There's the difference between us, Eric. I follow the truth.

SOLDIER Don't push it Regina.

REGINA Doctor Woolf to you. Eric, I feel you've served your purpose. Young Otto. Can you drive?

LITTLE OTTO Yes.

REGINA You've got a job. My assistant. Lead the way. Goodbye Eric.

LITTLE OTTO **Scene Four. The Institute.**

FRIEDA The Institute was a huge old building.
Inside it was all white walls.
Like a hospital.
Or a prison.

REGINA Welcome to the Institute. You won't feel the war here. We are dedicated to the pursuit of truth and a better world. In here we will rid the world of war, famine, illness and imperfection. You have stepped out of the past. You are now in the future. Outside are the ignorant, the backward looking. In here we look forward.

FRIEDA And we're safe here?

REGINA Oh yes.

FRIEDA What do you actually do here?

REGINA We study humans. Find out what makes them tick.

FRIEDA I expect you have ways of making us tock, as well.

REGINA	What?
FRIEDA	Don't worry. It's what I do. So where do we perform?
REGINA	Don't worry about that just yet. These are your rooms.
FRIEDA	Bars on the window.
REGINA	That's to stop people breaking in, not getting out. We're doing important research.
FRIEDA	Where are our costumes?
REGINA	I've arranged for new ones to be made. I'm expecting very important guests. I want you to look your best.
FRIEDA	The next day, they began to measure us. Every day we would be measured.

Scene Five. The secret of Eirwen.

	Little Otto gave us hospital gowns and watched as they measured me, Mum, Dad and took samples of our blood and saliva. Every bit of us was scanned and prodded. (*To LITTLE OTTO.*) What are you doing with her?
LITTLE OTTO	It's a job.
FRIEDA	But what's it all for?
REGINA	We study human beings here.
LITTLE OTTO	Why?
REGINA	To see how we can improve them.
LITTLE OTTO	How do you do that?
REGINA	We take tissue from humans and grow new humans.
LITTLE OTTO	Really?
REGINA	But improved humans.
LITTLE OTTO	That can't be done.

REGINA	It already has been.
OTTO	I'd like to see it.
REGINA	You already have. Here she is, Eirwen.
FRIEDA	I knew there was something weird about her.
REGINA	She is not in fact my daughter. But she is made from me. Though younger than me. She is my twin. But more perfect and more intelligent than I could ever be.
FRIEDA	What are you talking about?
REGINA	Look at her. Isn't she lovely?
BERTHA	If you wanted a baby why not just have one? It's easy enough. Most people have a problem stopping them.
REGINA	Well, as it happens I can't have children normally.
BERTHA	Oh, sorry.
REGINA	That's quite alright. But what's normal? Look at you? Are you normal?
BERTHA	Yes!
REGINA	Well then. You are in no position to judge me. I made her from a piece of me. She is my twin but vastly improved. I chose her attributes. She has beauty, intelligence, health, a long life.
	They look at EIRWEN.
LITTLE OTTO	So you really don't have parents.
OTTO	You weren't born.
BERTHA	You don't have a soul.
LITTLE OTTO	You're a clone.

FRIEDA	You were made in a laboratory. I always knew there was something strange about you.
OTTO	Snow white.
BERTHA	Ebony hair, white skin, ruby lips.
FRIEDA	Cold as ice.
LITTLE OTTO	Don't talk about her like that. You wouldn't like it.
FRIEDA	So we're not the only freaks here.
BERTHA	You're not a freak.
REGINA	And neither is my daughter. She's perfect.
BERTHA	This is not natural. It's wrong.
REGINA	People might say the same about you.
BERTHA	How dare you. This can't be legal.
REGINA	No, It's not. You are right. The government is not as forward-thinking as we might like. Which is why I needed to get her back. And I will not have her exposed to bigots like you.
BERTHA	We are not bigots. How could we be? We've been up against it all our lives.
REGINA	Just because you're short, you can't be small-minded?
BERTHA	No!
REGINA	Not very accepting though, are we? But you're right. The authorities would be very annoyed if they knew.
FRIEDA	We'll tell them.
REGINA	I don't think you are in any position to tell anyone anything.

FRIEDA	They kept on measuring us but we never saw our costumes and we never got to do the performance.

OTTO goes to REGINA.

Scene Six. Otto makes a proposal.

OTTO	A word?
REGINA	What is it Otto?
OTTO	You can really do this? Take a human and reproduce them?
REGINA	Oh yes.
OTTO	Good. I've got a proposal.
REGINA	Which is?
OTTO	Do it from me. Make another me. Or Bertha or Frieda. There's not enough dwarfs for our show. Make some more. This could be the answer. Do it. Come on. We'll be minted. I'll cut you into the show. Ten per cent. What do you say?
REGINA	Don't be ridiculous, my science is a boon to humanity.
OTTO	Exactly, so are we. We could have the whole country laughing.
REGINA	We are trying to eliminate defects.
OTTO	Defect?! We are not a defect.
REGINA	Then what are you?
OTTO	We are extraordinary, amazing. Evidence of the creativity of the universe. We are not some mistake. We are marvels. And we are not going to be eliminated.
REGINA	Oh yes you are.
OTTO	We'll see. But if it does happen, I tell you this.

REGINA	What?
OTTO	You'll miss us when we're gone.
FRIEDA	**Scene Seven. Little Otto shows a big heart.**
LITTLE OTTO	So here you are. Snow White, back in her palace.
EIRWEN	So what does that make you?
LITTLE OTTO	The Prince?
EIRWEN	You ran off with the evil queen the first chance you got.
LITTLE OTTO	Yeah. So what did Miss Perfect do here all day?
EIRWEN	Wander the empty corridors. Look through the bars.
LITTLE OTTO	Anyone to play with?
EIRWEN	No, just lots of lessons. And books to read.
LITTLE OTTO	Doesn't sound so bad.
EIRWEN	I'm a freak.
LITTLE OTTO	You're not a freak.
EIRWEN	I'm a clone. I've got no soul.
LITTLE OTTO	Oh you've got a soul alright. You're just a bit of a spoiled brat.
	EIRWEN starts to cry.
	Are you crying? Or just leaking hydraulic fluid?
EIRWEN	Why don't you just go away?
LITTLE OTTO	Sorry. You're definitely a human.
EIRWEN	No I'm not.
LITTLE OTTO	You've got feelings.
EIRWEN	Humans have families. I don't.

LITTLE OTTO	Families? They're more trouble than they're worth.
EIRWEN	Yours is the only family I've ever known. They don't seem so bad.
FRIEDA	**Scene Eight. I decide to make a break for it.**
LITTLE OTTO	Frieda.
FRIEDA	Otto. I have bad feelings about this place. I'm getting out.
LITTLE OTTO	Deserting the show? You?
FRIEDA	Don't tell on me.
LITTLE OTTO	I won't.
FRIEDA	Otto, why are you working for her?
LITTLE OTTO	What else is there?
FRIEDA	You're one of us.
LITTLE OTTO	No I'm not. I'm not us, I'm them now. Ask Dad.
FRIEDA	Come with me.
LITTLE OTTO	I can't.
FRIEDA	Then tell me what exactly goes on here?
LITTLE OTTO	I don't know.
FRIEDA	I've been checking it out. I keep thinking I'll come to a long corridor, somewhere with a secret door which is always kept locked.
LITTLE OTTO	You think?
FRIEDA	Mysterious sounds come from behind it. Nobody's allowed in.
LITTLE OTTO	And I expect you're looking for the way out Frieda, and you find yourself in the corridor.

FRIEDA   On my own?

LITTLE OTTO Naturally.

FRIEDA   And the door just happens to be unlocked.

LITTLE OTTO Of course. And you can't resist looking in it.
             And there is Regina. And she's leaning over a
             table.

FRIEDA   Laughing evilly.

LITTLE OTTO There are bubbling tubes all around and
             buzzes of electricity.

FRIEDA   And on the table there's a body laid out.

LITTLE OTTO And it's made of pieces of other bodies.

FRIEDA   And I push something over by accident.

LITTLE OTTO So she notices you. And she turns.

FRIEDA   Slowly.

LITTLE OTTO And really she's not beautiful. She's hideously
             ugly. And she says.

FRIEDA   Ah Frieda, you are just in time to share with
             me my greatest moment. I will create life.

LITTLE OTTO And she cackles.

FRIEDA   At last I will be one with the gods. And she
             cackles again.

LITTLE OTTO Twice. And then you say. 'You. You're mad.'

FRIEDA   You'll never get away with it.

REGINA   (*Has been listening.*) That's where you're wrong.
             You are the one who will never get away.

FRIEDA   I'm going.

REGINA   That door you're standing next to is the door
             to the outside world. It's not locked.

FRIEDA   I could go.

REGINA	Yes, but where would you go, dear? It's a big world out there and you are a small person. You would be caught. Then you would be interned and disappeared like all the others. The world out there is doing its best to get rid of people like you. Soon you will all be gone. You'll be safer here
FRIEDA	Frieda tries to leave, but fear defeats her.
REGINA	Lab rats don't have so bad a life. Little Otto, take her back to her room
	FRIEDA goes back to her room.
	Oh look. It's starting to snow.
EIRWEN	**Scene Nine. Mother and Daughter.**
REGINA	Eirwen? What's wrong?
EIRWEN	Little Otto…
REGINA	Has he upset you?
EIRWEN	No, not him. It's me.
REGINA	Come and sit in front of the mirror. Let me brush your hair. I used to do this when you were little.
EIRWEN	Did you? I don't remember. Mirror, mirror on the wall. Why did you make me?
REGINA	When I was young I lived for science. It ate me up. I spent days and nights trying to understand what made humans work. Then suddenly, one day. I found I wanted a child, but couldn't have one. And that ate me up too. So I used my science and I made you.

73

EIRWEN	So you're human too. But not me.
REGINA	Look in the mirror. Who is the fairest of them all? Lovelier by far than anything that has gone before. And cleverer. What's 964 multiplied by 12789?
EIRWEN	12,328,596.
REGINA	See?
EIRWEN	A calculator bought in any shop could do it. It's just a trick, like being shot from a cannon into a bowl of rice pudding.
REGINA	What?
EIRWEN	Something Otto said.
REGINA	I wanted you so much. I thought I'd die.
EIRWEN	I'm sure you did. I just wish you'd worked out what to do with me when you'd got me.
REGINA	You could live forever.
EIRWEN	You wanted me so that you would live forever. I don't want this. I don't want to be the future. Your future.
REGINA	I think you need something to keep you calm. Little Otto give her a sedative.
FRIEDA	**Scene Ten. The show.** The day finally came for the show. We were taken to the stage. We stood behind the curtain as we had so many times before. We could hear the murmur of the audience.
BERTHA	Where's our costumes?
OTTO	We won't be needing them.

BERTHA	But we're performing.
OTTO	No we're not. It's us they're interested in. They just want to look at us.
BERTHA	Otto. You knew?
	OTTO clearly did.
	You knew we would be on display? How could you?
OTTO	It was this or starve. Bertha.
BERTHA	What?
OTTO	Before we do this. Tell me something. Am I shortest? Out of me and Gustav, am I the shortest.
BERTHA	Oh Otto, does it matter now?
OTTO	It matters to me. It matters.
BERTHA	Yes, Otto. Yes, you are.
OTTO	Thank you, Bertha.
FRIEDA	And then the curtain rose.
REGINA	Ladies and Gentlemen. Once upon a time, everyone agreed that science was a good thing. Nowadays nobody trusts science. You are here today to witness the results of an experiment which will change the world. I would like to introduce the Frantz family. Humankind has infinite variation. Mr Frantz, would you step forward. Here you see what nature can produce if left to itself. It is in its nature to mutate.
	She demonstrates the following on him with a tape measure.

Each limb is in the same relationship as the average person. But much shorter. In certain cases. Frieda, the limbs are in proportion. There are many kinds of mutations which produce this and now we have it in our power to control this process. Look now ladies and gentlemen. The Frantz family may well be the last. Soon people with these defects will not be born.
Meet the future.

EIRWEN   (*Drugged up voice.*) I am the future.

REGINA   Created from my own tissue, yet modified to be perfect in every respect. Any mathematical problem she can solve in seconds, Her memory is vast.

She picks up a tape measure.

If this is a normal life span.
This will be hers. Four times as long.
Though this is yet to be tested we estimate her life span to be at least three hundred years, maybe longer.

At some point in this FRIEDA takes the tape. She starts to measure herself and this develops into a tap dance which then becomes more lyrical.

She is giving her final performance.

Stop this stupid dancing. Stop this now.

LITTLE OTTO steps forward.

He starts to sing/shout.

LITTLE OTTO   There's a great many things
In this big wide world
For which I'd give you thanks
(Big thanks)

REGINA   Stop this ridiculous performance.

Stop it, you little freak.

The others start to join in.

OTHERS   A wave from a boy
A smile from a girl
Or a key to open banks
(Fat chance)

CHORUS
But there's just one thing
You can kindly stuff
And that's what I'll now name
I'm not being funny
You can keep your money
We'll never never never never
Ever ever ever ever
Never be all the same.
(Again)
We'll never never never never
Ever ever ever ever
Never be all the same.
I'm not you
And you're not me
This isn't rocket science.
(No fear)
Some are short
And some are fat
And some are even giants.
(Not here)

FRIEDA   **Scene Eleven. A turn up for the books.**
Suddenly the room went silent. The doors at
the back of the room opened. Eric the soldier
was standing there. In his uniform. He was
clapping.

SOLDIER   Well, you do put on a good show.
My congratulations Regina.

REGINA   What do you want, Eric?

SOLDIER	This Institute is now under military protection.
REGINA	What are you doing?
SOLDIER	We are taking you over.
REGINA	Important discoveries are being made here.
SOLDIER	We know. And from now on you'll be using them for us.
REGINA	What do you mean?
SOLDIER	You can create a human being – a perfect human being.
REGINA	So?
SOLDIER	So your research will now be used to create people for us – soldiers. To make an army, an indestructible army.
REGINA	No. My research is for creation not destruction.
SOLDIER	Your research is for whatever the government says it's for.
REGINA	I will not have it.
SOLDIER	You know Regina, for an intelligent woman, you are surprisingly stupid about the way the world works. And you totally underestimated me, didn't you?
REGINA	How dare you?
SOLDIER	You should get out more.
EIRWEN	**Scene Twelve. Chaos and confusion.**
FRIEDA	Suddenly all the scientists in the audience ran for the doors. It was chaos.
OTTO	Come on we're going.
SAM	Frieda. Frieda. Let me carry you out.
FRIEDA	I'll be alright. You look after yourself.

SAM   Marry me.

FRIEDA   What?

SAM   I don't think I can say it again. It just sort of
              popped out. I didn't mean to say it.

FRIEDA   Marry you? Um, don't take this wrong but I
              don't think that would be a good idea.

SAM   I knew it. I'm too tall for you, aren't I?

FRIEDA   No. Really no. But you are too old.
              And I rather hoped I'd be in love when I got
              married. If I ever do.

SAM   Keep it in mind.

FRIEDA   I don't think I'll change on this one. You
              should get on with your life. It is after all too
              short. And I'm not.
              Come on Mum.

SAM   Quick this way.

FRIEDA   Was that true, about Dad being shortest?

BERTHA   No.

FRIEDA   Really? You lied?

BERTHA   Well sometimes love is more important than
              truth. Don't tell him.

LITTLE OTTO   (*Finds EIRWEN. She is laying unconscious.*) Eirwen.
              Eirwen wake up. We've got to go. Eirwen,
              come on. I'm not leaving you here. There's
              only one thing for it.

              *He gives her a big passionate kiss. EIRWEN comes
              round.*

EIRWEN   Where did you learn to kiss like that?

LITTLE OTTO   (*To audience.*) Fairy tales.
              (*To EIRWEN.*) Come with me.

EIRWEN   Where?

LITTLE OTTO	I don't know. Anywhere.
EIRWEN	Why? I'm a freak.
LITTLE OTTO	You don't want to stay one do you?
EIRWEN	No.
LITTLE OTTO	Then come on.
EIRWEN	No. Not that way, you'll be caught. I grew up in these corridors. Come on everyone, follow me. We need to get onto the roof.
FRIEDA	Is everybody here?
OTTO	Otto? Where's Otto?
LITTLE OTTO	I'm here. Dad. I didn't mean to grow. It just happened.
OTTO	I wanted you to look up to me. I wanted you to be one of us. Not one of them.
LITTLE OTTO	I'm still your son.
OTTO	I know. You've grown.
LITTLE OTTO	Sorry.
OTTO	No, grown up. That's nothing to do with your size. Come here. Give us a hug.
	They hug.
	Enough of that. Let's go.
REGINA	**Scene Thirteen. Oh dear.** You have my daughter. Eirwen. Come here.
EIRWEN	No.
REGINA	Come here.
EIRWEN	No. I want to go. I want to go with them.
REGINA	With them?
EIRWEN	Yes.

REGINA	Why?
EIRWEN	I like them. They're not perfect.
REGINA	But you are.
EIRWEN	No, I'm not. I'm just beautiful. I'm barely human.
REGINA	Human? Is that so great? They hate what they don't understand and start wars on the basis of it. Why would you want to be merely human, when you can be perfect?
EIRWEN	Did you ever read those stories you gave me? Snow White? Did you ever read it?
REGINA	No.
EIRWEN	Well now you'll have time.
REGINA	But what will happen to you? There's a war out there.
LITTLE OTTO	She'll be safer with us. If she stays here they won't let you keep her. They'll take her from you. She'll be a lab rat. A freak. With us she has a chance.
REGINA	Otto, you have destroyed my work, you little swine.
OTTO	What did you call me?
REGINA	I called you, if you didn't hear – a – little – swine.
OTTO	I may be a swine. I am in fact a swine. You are not wrong there. But the fact that I am little has nothing to do with it. I am little and I am a swine. I am a swine, but I am a big one. And so, madam, are you. You're not so different.
LITTLE OTTO	They're coming.

81

REGINA	(*To EIRWEN.*) Go then. (*To OTTO.*) Take her. And see if you can teach her how to be human.
OTTO	And now we're off. Thank you and good night.
FRIEDA	So we went. And we kept on going. We haven't really stopped since. We put as much distance as we could between us and the war. It's another story I'll have to tell you another time. And one night we slipped across a border into a place that wasn't at war. We came to a vast camp of refugees. So we started to create a new show.
LITTLE OTTO	I directed it.
EIRWEN	I wrote it.
SAM	I stage managed it.
BERTHA	I did the costumes.
OTTO	I put up with it.
FRIEDA	And I'm starring in it. It's not Snow White. It's called, 'Whiter than Snow'. And you just watched it. Then on the first night, this happened.

LITTLE OTTO and EIRWEN come to the others.

Scene Fourteen. News.

EIRWEN	Everybody. We've got some news.
OTTO	What's that, son?
LITTLE OTTO	We're getting married.

Big celebrations.

FRIEDA	Getting married!
BERTHA	Aw.
SAM	Congratulations.

BERTHA   I'll make your frock.

OTTO   Well done, son.

LITTLE OTTO   Wait. Wait. and…

EIRWEN   I'm having a baby.

BERTHA   A baby?

                A sudden silence falls.

SAM   Congratulations.

BERTHA   I'll let out your frock.

LITTLE OTTO   Thanks.

                LITTLE OTTO faces OTTO.

OTTO   Will it be…

BERTHA   Otto!

LITTLE OTTO   We don't know if it will be short or tall.

EIRWEN   It will be loved.

FRIEDA   It will be loved.

EIRWEN   And that will be enough.

FRIEDA   And they all lived happily ever after.
                As if…

                THE END

Credits

Cast

In order of appearance

Ezra **Amit Sharma**
Imaginary Dad/Dad **David Ellington**
Louise **Cherylee Houston**
Mum **Karen Spicer**

Other characters played by the cast are:

Spud
Imaginary Dad
The Bus Conductor
Ticket Officer
The Man

Creative Team

Writer **Mike Kenny**
Director **Jenny Sealey**
Designer **Lisa Ducie** (Renaissance Creative Design)
Lighting Design **Ian Scott**
Composer **James M Keane**

Diary of an Action Man was originally co-commissioned
by Graeae and Unicorn Theatre.

A Note from the Writer

Generally Jenny and I have always worked with the strengths and difficulties of the company at the time. Of course it's politics, a view that no one should be excluded, but it has also led us to produce some fascinating pieces of theatre. From the start in the 80s we began by incorporating signing into performances and I became adept at cutting extraneous talk. When it came to working on *Action Man* we had begun to look at incorporating audio description into the text. I found it really hard. After spending a career cutting out words, I was now looking for ways of putting them in.

There's little in this play that is specific to being disabled in any way. The play is not 'about' disability, nor does it use disability as a metaphor. One of the characters has a wheelchair that is referred to but that was mainly because the actress playing her used a wheelchair. The issues that occur in this family are not to do with their being disabled.

Much of theatre works on subtext. How do blind people access this? Obviously, the primary way in has to be through text. There is a huge tension in realising this. I found it hard to achieve, to write a theatre piece not a radio play. I chose many different tactics as you'll see, and I was pretty pleased with the results; however what I came up with was something that works for this particular play, I didn't come up with a handy check list for future projects. The search continues.

Mike Kenny 2009

A Note from the Director

Background to the commission

Mike and I had two ideas for the play. One was an interest in invisible friends; the other was an interest in the relationship between boys and their dads. Mike had already written me a play about a mother and daughter (*Stepping Stones*) and an opera about sisters (*Mad Meg*). He is a dad to three boys so the time was right to tackle the complex relationships between father and son.

Often Dad isn't around as much as Mum and boys are very hazy about what they're for. Men are often characterised in the media as heroes or a 'waste of space' and fathers are represented by Homer Simpson. Since this play was written, the country has once again been at war; the concept of heroism is back in currency and men are needed again.

The Play

Diary of an Action Man is about boys and their fathers, and the difficult journey from boy to man. When our play begins we seem to be looking at an ideal family on a normal day. Dad is a soldier. Only at the end of the first scene does the penny drop; the father exists only in the boy's head.

The son believes his real father died a hero, and has a close and warm relationship with his imaginary dad, who is everything a son could want. It comes as a surprise when he discovers that his father isn't in fact dead and he goes with his imaginary dad on a search to find him. The real dad is quite a different animal. He doesn't want to be found. He's not a hero, he ran away and the play examines the process of the son coming to terms with his real father, a human being.

Style

This was first performed by an integrated cast of disabled and non-disabled actors. The narrative style is in a diary form which allows Ezra to be very descriptive about what he is doing. His mum, sister and friend all copy his way of communicating. This style gives Blind and Visually Impaired audiences access to the play. Deaf children have access through the relationship between the imaginary dad and his son who communicate in a secret coded language borrowed from British Sign Language and gestural language. The issues of access are woven into the fabric of the script so it becomes a play for all children to own.

When we were developing the play we did not realise that Real Dad would be deaf. Imaginary Dad signed because he had to have a secret language with his children. When we got to the scenes with Real Dad it became obvious to us that he was deaf and that is why his children signed and mum did not. Mum did not like being reminded of signing as that made her think of her ex-husband.

Playing around with descriptive and signed access is always exciting and we found out things we may never have done if access was not an important issue for Graeae and our plays.

Jenny Sealey 2009

Biographies

Amit Sharma Ezra

Amit is a graduate of Graeae's *Missing Piece 1* training course. As well as acting for Graeae he is an Associate Artist for the company and a member of the very first Ensemble created at the Unicorn. Amit has gone on to work as a writer, actor, director and television presenter.

Who was your superhero?

"I was (still am) football mad. Gabriel Batistuta of Argentina. He was a goal machine. The way he would score goals with such ease and grace had me transfixed to the television set whenever 'Bati-Gol', his nickname, played. I tried to copy the way he celebrated, the way he walked around the pitch, even my unsuccessful attempt to grow long hair like him. He's my superhero."

David Ellington Imaginary Dad/Dad

Bristol born David's roles have been diverse, including film, theatre and television drama and presenting. David is also a Graeae Associate Artist, a board member of DRoots Theatre and a director of VS1 Productions. David's other creative work includes the Film Club for Deaf children, co-producing deaf comedy and thriller short films and he has also supported ALRA in running theatre courses for Deaf students.

Who was your superhero?

"*Batman* because he is energetic, a strategic thinker and stubborn. He likes to challenge the dark sides in order to make a comfortable life for human beings. He often encounters and tackles the unsolved, mysterious situations to rescue someone who is trapped inside."

Cherylee Houston Louise

Cherylee has toured several times with Graeae. TV roles include: Belle Hutchinson in *Doctors* and Dorothy in *I'm with Stupid*; other credits include *Holby City*, *The Bill* and *Little Britain*.

Who was your superhero?

"My mum was my superhero, she made coloured lemonade by magic and told me anything is possible if you set your mind to it. If I could be a super hero I would be Glitter Lady, who makes everything glittery as you can't be sad if you can sparkle."

Karen Spicer Mum & Other Characters

Many moons ago Karen played daughters: she was the original Cynth in Jenny Sealey's award-winning production of Mike Kenny's *Stepping Stones*. Since then she has gone on to play mums for companies including Graeae, Red Ladder, Nottingham Roundabout and Fittings Multi-Media Arts. She has also been TV mums, social workers, lawyers and teachers in *Coronation Street*, *Emmerdale*, *Doctors*, *No Angels*, *The Royal*, *The Royal Today*, *Heartbeat* and *Clocking Off*.

Who was your superhero?

"My Super Hero was *Wonder Woman*, because she was fighting for our rights in her sparkly tights... Wonder Woman that is, not Karen."

Lisa Ducie Designer

Lisa is now part of a design company Renaissance Creative Design based in Brighton, producing bespoke bridal and occasion wear for individual clients. They also design extravagant events for clients including the O2 Dome, Royal Albert Hall, Kensington Palace, BBC and Trafalgar Square festivals.

James M Keane Composer

James trained at Trinity College of Music. He has composed for theatre, dance, TV, animation and the concert hall and has conducted music for opera (*Newsnight the Opera*, BAC; *The Silver Swan*, ROH), television (*Vanity Fair* BBC; *Queer as Folk* C4), film, CD, concerts and has conducted and performed for the Clod Ensemble's installation concerts and music theatre production. He lectures in Theatre Improvisation at University College Winchester.

Ian Scott Lighting Designer

Ian has collaborated on many Graeae productions including *Fittings: The Last Freak Show, The Fall of the House of Usher, Peeling, Bent* and *Blasted*. Most recently Ian designed the set and lighting for *Static*, a co-production with Suspect Culture.

The Unicorn Theatre is one of the leading producers of professional theatre for children and young people in the UK. Situated on the south bank of the Thames, it is the only purpose-built theatre for young people in London.

The Unicorn was originally set up in 1947 by Caryl Jenner, and started its journey as a small touring company operating from the back of an army surplus van and playing to young audiences of post-war Britain. It has since grown to become the country's flagship theatre for young people.

In 2005, the Unicorn moved to its new home near London Bridge. It comprises two theatre spaces (the Weston Theatre and the Clore Theatre), education studio, café and other welcoming areas for families and schools.

Characters

EZRA

LOUISE
Ezra's Little Sister

MUM

IMAGINARY DAD / REAL DAD

SPUD
Ezra's Friend

Other Characters in Part Two:

THE BUS CONDUCTER

THE GIRL

TICKET OFFICER

THE MAN

The dialogue in this play incorporates some stage directions. Where stage directions are not to be spoken they are in Italics.

Part One

EZRA's bedroom. An attic room, or maybe just a very small room.
Toys everywhere. It should look like total chaos out of which order will
emerge.

There are lots of toys that relate to going on journeys.

DAD is somewhere in the room, possibly high up on a bunkbed.

EZRA appears in a spotlight or torchlight, full of energy.

EZRA   September 7th 2003, 15:00 hours
      Ezra's sitting in his bedroom.
      In the dark.
      Outside the sun's shining
      He's got the curtains closed.
      His stuff laid out.
      Check
      Cars, check
      Action men, check.
      Dinosaurs, check
      Lego, check
      Guns, check
      Train, check
      Barbie
      Barbie?
      What's that doing in here?
      Louise.
      I'll kill her.

      Right
      The story.
      Dad?
      Dad?
      Where are you?

      A light flicks up on DAD.

      Dad.
      My dad's a soldier

He was a hero.

DAD looks modest.

He fought in the war.
He was very brave, weren't you?

DAD looks modest.

He doesn't like to talk about it.
Was it very scary?

DAD   I don't like to talk about it.
       Tell the story.

EZRA   Thing about stories
       You need a good start.
       This story starts in the dark.
       You see nothing
       You just hear
       The sound of
       A helicopter.
       No, a car
       No, a helicopter

DAD   Good start.

EZRA   You need a good ending too.

DAD   Worry about that later.

EZRA   Question: The most rubbish ending for a story?

DAD   'They all lived happily ever after?'

EZRA   Wrong.
       'And I woke up and it was all a dream.'
       Rubbish.
       So, September 7th 2003, 15:05
       Boy's crossing a field.
       Mobile phone falls from the helicopter.
       He catches it.
       He answers it.
       Dad?
       What are you doing?

DAD signs and EZRA interprets. It's as if they're creating the story together.

The enemy?
Where?
Behind enemy lines
Are they coming to save you?
Why not?
You're on a secret mission.
They've washed their hands of you.
The phone goes dead.
Dad?
Dad?
September 7th 2003, 15:00 hours
Ezra's on a mission:
'Save Dad'.

To DAD.

Stay up there Dad.
I'm coming to get you.
Hang on.

DAD   Is it finished?

EZRA   Course it's not finished.
            It's only just started.

DAD   What happens?

EZRA   I don't know what happens yet.
            A good story doesn't tell you everything at once.
            There's got to be a few surprises.

DAD   Go on then surprise me.

EZRA   Right.
            All this stuff looks like toys, right?

DAD   Right.

EZRA   Wrong.
            It's in disguise.

DAD   All of it?

EZRA   Nothing is what it seems.

Ezra picks up a comic.
Looks like a comic, right?

DAD   Right.

EZRA   Wrong.
It's a message.

DAD   Who from?

EZRA   You

It says
Don't believe everything you're told.
I'm telling you now, so you know.
So don't blame me.
'cos I've told you now.
That's the one thing you should believe.
You can't believe everything you're told.
Trust no one.
September 7th 2003, 15:15
Ezra prepares.

Weapons, check.
Supplies, check
Map, check
Disguises, check
Rope, check.

He collects most of his toys. His mission will be in a mixture of scales.

Ready.
I'm coming Dad.

He picks up a dinosaur.

Ezra picks up a dinosaur.
Louise? What are you doing here?
'I want to come.'
You can't.
You're too young.
Go back. Look after Mum.
'But I want to.'
Well you can't.

DIARY OF AN ACTION MAN

Shut up.
Ezra throws her away.
Don't worry, Dad
I'm on my way.
Just stay there.
September 7th 2003, 15:17
They're everywhere
Walking their dogs.
Pushing their buggies.
And you can't tell who's on their side just by
looking.
How do I tell, Dad?
Some of them look like ordinary people.

DAD   Trust no one.
Check the area.
Now go, go, go!
Ezra runs, dodging in and out of the people.
He ducks into the station.
Slows down.
Lose them in the crowd.
They won't try anything here.

EZRA   He's going by train.
Ezra picks up the train carefully.
This used to be yours, didn't it Dad?
That's why it looks dead old.
It doesn't work any more.
It's an antique.

DAD   Be careful with it.

EZRA   I am careful with it.

DAD   Look after it for me.

EZRA   I will Dad.
Don't worry.
On the train.
Made it.

Train rhythm.

Rocking.

I'm getting my dad
I'm coming to save him
They've got him
They've got him
His life's in danger

DAD   Ezra, look out.
They're coming down the train.

EZRA   They know I'm here.
They're getting closer.
They're getting closer.
They're after me.
They're going to get me.
Dad, what shall I do?

His younger sister, LOUISE, sticks her head round the door.

LOUISE   Ezra's little sister, Louise, sticks her head round the door. She's in a wheelchair. She's very pretty. And popular.

EZRA   No you're not.
Push off.

LOUISE   Louise looks around Ezra's room.
She sees more than she says.

EZRA   Ezra wastes her.

He guns her down.

LOUISE   What you doing, Ezra?

EZRA   Go away.

LOUISE   You playing?

EZRA   No. Go away.

LOUISE   Can I play?

EZRA   No.

LOUISE   I'll tell Mum.

EZRA   Go on, tell her.

LOUISE   I will.

	I'll tell her you're playing with guns.
EZRA	So?
LOUISE	You know she doesn't like it.
EZRA	Go on then.
LOUISE	I will.
EZRA	She won't.
LOUISE	She will. You don't want to believe everything he tells you. *She goes.*
EZRA	Ezra's sister goes. She's ugly. And nobody likes her.
DAD	Are you coming?
EZRA	Yeah. Stay there Dad. I'm still coming. September 7th 2003, 15:20 They're after me. What do I do Dad?
DAD	Out of the window. Up on the roof of the train.
EZRA	They'll never find me here. Suddenly, we go into a tunnel. *The lights all go on and we see EZRA's room. His MOTHER is there.*
MUM	Ezra's mum arrives. She turns on the lights. Ezra!
EZRA	Ezra hides the gun. Mum doesn't notice.
MUM	Yes she does. Mum looks at the room. She looks tired.
EZRA	Ezra doesn't notice.

MUM   Yes he does.
        On her face is a smile.

EZRA   But it's just teeth.

MUM   Oh, look at the mess.

EZRA   What mess?

MUM   This.
        This room.

EZRA   It's not a mess.

MUM   Look at it.

EZRA   No.

MUM   How do you find anything?
        She picks up his train.

EZRA   Don't.
        Don't touch it
        You'll break it.
        Don't move it.
        It's not a mess.
        I know where everything is.

MUM   She puts down the train.

EZRA   Ezra picks it up.

MUM   Ezra.
        It's a mess
        And it needs tidying
        And I don't want to do it.

EZRA   Well don't then.

MUM   Ezra.
        What are you doing anyway?

EZRA   Nothing.

MUM   Why don't you go out?

EZRA   I'm busy.

MUM   It's a lovely sunny day out there.

EZRA   No.

MUM	Ezra,
	Be nice.
	Just for today.
	And play with your sister.
EZRA	No.
MUM	Just for a bit.
	While I make tea.
EZRA	She spoils everything.
MUM	Please.
EZRA	She does.
MUM	Just for a bit.
EZRA	He looks away from her.
	Later.
MUM	Thanks.
	She looks away from him.
	There's someone coming for tea.
	Be nice.
	She goes.
EZRA	So where was I?
DAD	In the tunnel.
EZRA	Yeah.
	Ezra's clinging to the roof of the train.
	Thundering through the dark.
	And I'm jumping off
	And rolling down the bank.
	I'm stealing an aeroplane.
	No, a helicopter.
	And I get to the mountain.
	Don't worry Dad.
	I'm nearly there.
	I climb the mountain
	Along the ledge.
	Louise, what are you doing here?
	Out of my way.

No!
I've got to get to Dad.
Dad.

DAD   What?

EZRA   Tell her.
Who do you love best?
Me or her?
Tell her.

DAD   You. Of course.

EZRA   See
He loves me best.
Me.
AAAARGH
She plummets.
To her death.
Ezra reaches his dad.
I'll get you out of this.
We're going home.
Ezra starts to untie his dad
Then suddenly he realises
They're not alone.
He turns round slowly
And sees
My arch enemy
Mirror Man.
Has he seen me?
Yes.
Long time no see, Mirror Man.
I should have known you were behind this.

He draws a gun.

Fast.
But not fast enough.
Ezra wastes him.

He grabs his dad.
Come on, Dad.
Home.

And they blast their way out.
Side by side.

They trash the room in the course of blasting their way out.

The end.

DAD   Brilliant.

EZRA   Have some crisps.
            Dad
            If I was captured
            You'd come and get me wouldn't you?

DAD   Of course I would.

EZRA   This is my dad.
            Say hallo, Dad.

DAD   Hallo Dad.

EZRA   He thinks he's funny.

DAD   I think I'm funny.

EZRA   Well, you're not.
            Do you know what's the most rubbish ending for
            a story?

DAD   'I woke up and it was all a dream.'

EZRA   Yeah.
            It does my head in.
            That is the most most rubbishest ending for a
            story
            Don't you think?
            Spud, right,
            He did this story at school, right.
            And it was a good story, and he was surrounded.
            No way up
            No way down.
            Surrounded.
            He couldn't get out, right.
            And then he says
            And I woke up and it was all a dream.

I mean, rubbish.
And the teacher still read it out.
That is so rubbish.
And she must have known.
You can't trust anyone.
It does my head in.
She only read it out 'cos his mum's mad.
He should have just mowed them all down.
Rubbish.
That's what you would've done, right?

LOUISE   Louise arrives.

EZRA   Push off.

LOUISE   Mum says tea's in five minutes
And you've got to play with me.

EZRA   Give us a go in your chair.

LOUISE   Give us a go with your train.

EZRA   No way.

LOUISE   Your gun then.

EZRA   Thinks about it.

LOUISE   Well?

EZRA   I'm thinking about it.

LOUISE   Louise sighs.

EZRA   Go on then.

LOUISE   Louise lets him.

EZRA   Reluctantly.
But don't touch anything else.
Lego.
You can touch the Lego
Not the red bits.

LOUISE   Louise starts to build a house.
What are you doing?

EZRA   Sorting this stuff out.

LOUISE   It's a mess.

EZRA	Now it is.
	Ezra puts everything back where it was.
	The action men go…
LOUISE	She's asked somebody to tea.
DAD	Who?
EZRA	Who?
	The guns go…
LOUISE	Somebody called Rob.
DAD	Why?
EZRA	Why?
LOUISE	She wants us to meet him.
DAD	Why?
EZRA	Why?
LOUISE	She says he's nice.
DAD	Nice, eh?
EZRA	And the train goes…
	Ezra stops.
	Who is he?
LOUISE	I don't know.
	She says he's nice.
EZRA	I'm not meeting him.
SPUD	Ezra's friend Spud arrives.
LOUISE	He walks into the room as if he expects to be chucked out.
SPUD	Your mum sent me in.
	You coming out?
EZRA	No.
SPUD	I haven't got long.
	My mum…
	He looks around the room.
EZRA	She still mad?

SPUD	She's not mad she's clinically depressed and she can't go out.
EZRA	What's stopping her?
SPUD	Don't know.
EZRA	She could if she wanted to.
LOUISE	You don't go out much either.
EZRA	That's different.
LOUISE	Why?
EZRA	Shut up Louise.
LOUISE	You haven't been out for weeks and weeks.
EZRA	I go to school, don't I?
SPUD	Spud looks at Louise. Hiya, Louise
LOUISE	Hiya.
SPUD	Nice chair.
LOUISE	Thanks.
SPUD	Can I have a go?
LOUISE	No.
SPUD	I'll give you a Mars bar. I've got loads.
LOUISE	Don't like them. What else have you got?
SPUD	Nothing. Met this bloke in the kitchen.
LOUISE	That's Rob.
SPUD	Is he your dad?
LOUISE	No.
SPUD	He seems to like your mum.
EZRA	Does he?
SPUD	She seems to like him too.

	Are you coming out?
EZRA	No.
SPUD	She was kissing him so I thought he must be your dad.
EZRA	Well he's not.
	Our dad's dead.
	That's your next surprise.
	I'm the only one who can see him.
	You weren't expecting that, were you?
LOUISE	Louise gives Ezra a look.
EZRA	What are you looking at?
	Our dad's dead, isn't he Louise?
LOUISE	Yeah.
SPUD	Oh,
	Sorry.
EZRA	He was a soldier
	He was a hero
	He fought in the war
	He was very brave, wasn't he Louise?
LOUISE	Louise looks at the floor
EZRA	She doesn't like to talk about it.
	He was rescuing his friend.
	It was very scary
	But he never cried, did he Louise?
LOUISE	Louise doesn't look at him.
	No.
SPUD	What war?
EZRA	What?
SPUD	What war?
	There isn't a war.
EZRA	There's always a war somewhere.
	It was a secret war.
	They don't tell you everything, you know.

	Stupid.
	See this.
	It was his train when he was a boy
	It's mine now.
	It's very valuable.
SPUD	Spud doesn't know what to say.
	He looks at the train.
	Its wheels are broken.
EZRA	That's because it's an antique.
	Go away now, I've got to sort out my stuff.
SPUD	Spud doesn't move.
	He looks at Louise.
LOUISE	No help there.
EZRA	Go on, time to wake up.
	This is all a dream.
SPUD	What?
LOUISE	Bye.
SPUD	See you later.
EZRA	Yeah.
	He means no.
LOUISE	How's your mum?
SPUD	I'd better go.
	I've got to do the shopping.
	Spud goes.
LOUISE	Spud's gone.
	He's supposed to be your friend.
EZRA	He is.
LOUISE	You're not very nice to him.
EZRA	That's what friends are for.
	Ezra carries on sorting out his stuff.
	His dad helps him.
LOUISE	Louise plays with the Lego.

EZRA	She doesn't speak to Ezra.
LOUISE	And he doesn't speak to her.
MUM	Mum comes in again. Tea's ready.
LOUISE	What is it?
MUM	Come and see.
EZRA	You've got make up on.
MUM	Have I?
EZRA	Why?
MUM	Just felt like a change. Put your train down. I've got someone for you to meet.
EZRA	No. Who?
MUM	His name's Rob. Give it to me then. She takes it from him.
EZRA	Give it back. I don't want to meet him. Who is he?
MUM	Just a friend. Give him a chance. He's nice. Mum looks at the train.
EZRA	Mum's not looking at Ezra. Don't care. Don't want to meet him. Ezra goes to the door. I DON'T WANT TO MEET YOU!
MUM	Ezra, ssh! Louise, go and get your tea.
EZRA	He's not my dad YOU'RE NOT MY DAD.

AND I DON'T WANT TO MEET YOU!

He picks up a toy gun and machine guns the door.

And I don't have to, if I don't want to.

LOUISE	Louise hasn't moved.
MUM	Ezra, ssh! He's just a friend.
LOUISE	Mum's still not looking at Ezra
EZRA	YOU'RE NOT MY FRIEND.
MUM	He could maybe mend this. He's good with his hands.
LOUISE	She shouldn't have said that.
EZRA	NO. MY DAD'S GOING TO GET YOU. HE'LL KILL YOU.

More machine gunning.

MUM	Ezra, your dad's gone. I can't bring him back, even if I wanted to.
LOUISE	Mum.
MUM	Not now, Louise.
LOUISE	Mum.
MUM	Not now.
LOUISE	Ezra said Dad was dead.
EZRA	I'll kill you, Louise.
LOUISE	He told Spud that Dad was dead.
MUM	What?
EZRA	I'll kill you.
LOUISE	He isn't dead is he?
MUM	Ezra, your dad isn't dead.
LOUISE	He sent me a birthday card.
MUM	You know he isn't dead.

	He lives in Manchester.
	Why do you tell these stories?
LOUISE	I knew you were lying.
EZRA	He is dead.
MUM	He isn't.
EZRA	Then why isn't he here?
MUM	Well…
LOUISE	Louise looks through the window.
	Rob's off.
MUM	What?
EZRA	Good.
LOUISE	He's going.
EZRA	He's scared of Dad.
MUM	Mum runs to the window.
	Rob, no!
EZRA	Ezra guns him down.
LOUISE	In the back?
MUM	You little…
	Look what you've done
	Look what you've done now.
EZRA	I'm glad.
MUM	I'm going to get him back
	And you're going to say sorry.
EZRA	You wouldn't get Dad back
	Go and get Dad back.
	I'm not saying anything to him.
MUM	Tidy this stuff up.
EZRA	'Cos he's dead.
MUM	He's not.
LOUISE	Mum starts to tidy up
EZRA	He wouldn't just leave us.

	And not get in touch.
MUM	Well he did.
EZRA	He must be dead.
MUM	Ezra! He's not dead! He just left.
LOUISE	Mum's putting everything away.
EZRA	You're not telling us.
MUM	Enough. Enough now. I can't make your dad come back.
LOUISE	Mum's putting everything in boxes.
EZRA	Why?
MUM	Ask him, not me.
EZRA	How can I?
MUM	He just walked out. He never said.
LOUISE	Mum's packing everything away.
EZRA	Ezra picks up the train. He wouldn't have left this. Why didn't he take it?
MUM	I don't know. Maybe he didn't want it.
EZRA	He wouldn't.
MUM	Obviously he didn't want us.
LOUISE	Mum's looking out the window. She's trying not to cry.
EZRA	Ezra doesn't say anything.
MUM	I knew he was a soldier when I married him. I knew one day he might have to fight. I didn't know we'd end up fighting each other.
EZRA	You didn't love him.

MUM	Ezra.
	I know it's not exciting but he lives in Manchester.
	I've washed my hands of him.
LOUISE	Mum puts the last toy in a box.
	She looks in the mirror.
MUM	Look at me now.
	I'm a mess.
	And I wanted it to be nice.
	I'm going after Rob.
LOUISE	Louise looks at Ezra.
EZRA	What?
LOUISE	Nothing.
	She keeps looking at him.
EZRA	What?
LOUISE	Nothing.
EZRA	Mum loves you better than she does me.
LOUISE	It's because I'm a girl.
EZRA	It's 'cos of your operations.
LOUISE	I can't help that.
EZRA	Swap you.
LOUISE	No thanks.
	Do you remember Dad?
EZRA	Course I do.
LOUISE	I don't.
	She goes.
	EZRA on his own.
	He's not making contact with the audience.
	He's feeling guilty about lying to the audience.
EZRA	September 8th 2003, 05:50
	Ezra's still in his bedroom
	It's night time

Everybody's asleep
His stuff is all packed away.

Sorry.
I did warn you.
Trust no one.
Not even me.
I'm always telling stories.
It's not all lies.
Dad?
Dad, where are you?
He really was a soldier.
Weren't you?
And this was his train.
It doesn't work.

Come home, Dad.
Please come home.
Mum's got a boyfriend
Rob.
You better come home soon.
What are you doing in Manchester?

Stay there
Stay there, Dad.
I'm coming to find you.
I'm really coming to find you.
September 7th 2003, 15:15
Ezra's on a mission.

This is the story of Ezra's mission.
To rescue his dad.

*This section of the story is led by DAD; as it goes on he
becomes more and more of an action man.*

Ezra gets out of bed and gets dressed quickly
What will I need?
Supplies.
Disguise.
Weapons.
It's still dark

	He creeps to the door.
	He listens.
DAD	Don't forget the train.
EZRA	The train.
	The train.
	I've got to bring it.
	He creeps out of the door
	Down the landing.
	He unlocks it
	Quietly
	He pulls the bolt.
	Carefully
	Then suddenly he realises
	They're not alone.
	He turns round slowly
	And sees
	Louise? What are you doing here?
LOUISE	Where are you going?
EZRA	Nowhere. Go back to bed.
LOUISE	She doesn't.
EZRA	I'm on a secret mission.
	The government needs me.
LOUISE	Louise still doesn't move.
	Are you running away?
EZRA	No.
	I'm going to get Dad.
LOUISE	I want to come.
EZRA	You can't.
	You're too young.
	Go back. Look after Mum.
LOUISE	But I want to.
EZRA	Well you can't.
	Shut up.
LOUISE	He's my dad too.

EZRA	Somebody's got to look after Mum.
	Tell her I went round early to Spuds,
	I let him copy my homework.
LOUISE	She'll never believe that.
	She's not stupid.
EZRA	Well make up something better.
LOUISE	Ez, I'm not you.
	If she asks me I'll have to tell the truth.
EZRA	Look, I've got to go.
LOUISE	Louise holds out an envelope to him.
EZRA	What's that?
LOUISE	My birthday card from Dad.
EZRA	I don't want that.
LOUISE	It's got his address on.
	You'll need it.
EZRA	Ezra takes it from her.
	Thanks.
LOUISE	Good luck.
EZRA	See you.
	And Ezra slips through the door and out.
	It's nearly morning.
	Nobody around.
	Right Dad.
	Where are we going?
DAD	Follow me.
	Keep in the shadows.
	Down the entry
	Fast.
	Go, go, go!
	Stop.
	Look around the corner
	Anybody about?
	No.
	Run.

Over the fence.
Keep down.
Round the rec
Through the hedge.
Dog.
Big dog.
Keep calm.
Let him sniff you.
Move slowly and calmly.
Careful.
Over the fence.
Good
Now down.
On your belly.
Make sure nobody from the houses can see you.
Good.
So far.

EZRA   What now Dad?
        How do we get to Manchester?

DAD   Steal a helicopter.

EZRA   A helicopter?

DAD   Yes.

EZRA   I don't know where to find one.

DAD   Car then.

EZRA   Dad.

DAD   What?

EZRA   I can't drive.
        And I'd get seen.
        I'm only ten.

DAD   Bus?

EZRA   Bus.
        Dad.

DAD   What?

EZRA   No money.

DAD	Go home then?
EZRA	Home? I can't go home. So I go to Spud's. He lives in the flats. I knock on his bedroom window. Spud. Spud, wake up.
SPUD	Spud opens the window. Ezra, you're out?
EZRA	I need your help. I'm on a mission I've got to save my dad.
SPUD	I thought he was dead.
EZRA	So did I, but he's not. They've got him.
SPUD	Where?
EZRA	Manchester.
SPUD	I'm dreaming this aren't I? I'll wake up in a minute.
EZRA	Ezra punches him.
SPUD	Ow.
EZRA	I've got no money. You'll have to come with me.
SPUD	I can't go to Manchester. Who'll look after my mum?
EZRA	Lend me some then.
SPUD	I haven't got any.
EZRA	Yes you have. I know you have. You do the shopping.
SPUD	No.
EZRA	I'll give it back.

	My dad's rich. He's got five cars And a helicopter.
SPUD	I can let you have a fiver.
EZRA	Thanks Spud. Right, you never saw me. A voice calls Spud's name from inside the flat.
SPUD	My mum. I've got to go. Good luck.
EZRA	Ezra turns to go.
SPUD	Ez.
EZRA	What?
SPUD	How're you getting there?
EZRA	Train. See you.
SPUD	See you. Spud turns to go.
EZRA	Spud.
SPUD	What?
EZRA	Where does the Manchester train go from?
SPUD	Euston. Spud closes the window.
EZRA	Ezra and his dad get to the bus. It's getting light. Anybody around?
DAD	No. Disguise.
EZRA	Ezra puts on his sunglasses. The bus comes. Ezra's on the bus.
DRIVER	Where you going?

EZRA	Euston Station.
DRIVER	£1.20.
EZRA	Can you tell me when we get there?
DRIVER	You can't miss it.
EZRA	I'm blind.
DRIVER	Where's your dog?
EZRA	I'm allergic.
DRIVER	Should you be out on your own?
EZRA	My dad's meeting me there.
DRIVER	Get on.
EZRA	Thanks.
DAD	Dad hides under the seat.
EZRA	Dad, what are you doing?
DAD	They might see me.
EZRA	We get to the station.
DAD	Are we being followed?
EZRA	Looks around. Don't know.
DAD	Trust no one. They're everywhere Walking their dogs. Pushing their buggies And you can't tell who's on their side just by looking.
EZRA	How do I tell, Dad? Some of them look like ordinary people.
DAD	Trust no one. Check the area. Now go, go, go!
EZRA	Ezra runs, dodging in and out of the people. He ducks into the station. Slows down.

Lose them in the crowd.
They won't try anything here.

DAD   Into the gents.
Change your appearance.
Take off your jumper.
Lose the glasses.
Ready?

EZRA   Yes.

DAD   Let's go.
Oh no.

EZRA   What?

DAD   The barrier.

EZRA   And I haven't got a ticket.
Which train?
Which train?
I look around.
Oh no.

POLICE   You all right, sonny?

EZRA   A policeman.
Yes thanks.

POLICE   You look a bit lost.

EZRA   I'm just waiting for my mum.
She's taken my little sister to the toilet.
Oh, there she is over there.
Goodbye.

DAD   Close one.

EZRA   Ezra walks over to a woman with two kids and a
buggy who's just going through the barrier.
Let me help you with that.
You're welcome.

DAD   On the train.
Made it.

High fives his DAD.

EZRA	Now Ezra's on the train. Next to his dad. Ezra's sitting by the family that he walked through the barrier with. A little girl sits opposite him. She keeps looking at him. So does her mum.
WOMAN	Thanks for your help.
EZRA	That's alright.
WOMAN	What's your name?
EZRA	The name's Bond.
WOMAN	The woman looks at him. Bond?
EZRA	Ezra looks back at her. Yeah, Spud Bond.
WOMAN	Oh?
EZRA	When I was a baby I looked like a potato.
WOMAN	You travelling alone?
EZRA	No, my dad's with me.
WOMAN	He'd better hurry up or he'll miss the train.
EZRA	He's the driver.
WOMAN	Really? How interesting. So you lucky boy get to go lots of places.
EZRA	Oh yeah. I've been everywhere, nearly. I've been to Scotland And lots of places like that. He used to be a soldier. We lived all over the world.
WOMAN	Where.

EZRA	Everywhere. I've never been to Manchester.
WOMAN	Doesn't your mum ever come?
EZRA	No. She's clinically depressed. She doesn't leave the house.
WOMAN	How sad.
EZRA	Yes it is sad. The woman gives me a packet of crisps.

Train rhythm.

Rocking.

I'm getting my dad
I'm coming to save him
They've got him
They've got him
His life's in danger
The woman goes
The girl's still looking.

EZRA	Suddenly the guard arrives.
GUARD	Tickets please.
GIRL	My mum's got them. She's just down there.
GUARD	The guard looks at Ezra.
EZRA	Ezra looks out of the window.
GUARD	Tickets please.
EZRA	Ezra looks out of the window.
GUARD	Sonny. Tickets The guard touches Ezra's arm.
EZRA	Looks surprised.
GUARD	Tickets.
EZRA	Sorry, I'm deaf Deaf.

GUARD   (*Loud and slow.*) Tick-ets.

EZRA   My dad's got them.
He's down there.

GUARD   Sorry son.

EZRA   That's alright.

GIRL   The girl looks at him.
You're not deaf.

EZRA   Shall I tell you the truth?

GIRL   Yeah.

EZRA   My dad's on a secret mission.
I've got to get to him in Manchester
But there's a problem.

GIRL   What?

EZRA   All the guards on the train are agents for the
enemy.
They mustn't find me.

GIRL   I don't believe you.

EZRA   It's true.
They've got the real ones tied up in the guards'
van.

GIRL   Liar.

EZRA   I'll prove it.
Their uniforms don't fit very well, do they?

GIRL   No.

EZRA   That's because they stole them.

GIRL   You'll never get away.
They count everybody on the train
They'll know.

EZRA   They're coming down the train.
They know I'm here.
They're getting closer.
They're getting closer
They're after me.

	They're going to get me.
GIRL	I'll help. You go, I'll stop them. I can do this whenever I want to.
EZRA	What?
GIRL	I'm going to be sick.
EZRA	Thanks Dad, what shall I do?
DAD	Follow me.
EZRA	Ezra and his dad go down the train. They can't go any further. Dad, what shall I do?
DAD	Right, on the roof.
EZRA	On the roof?
DAD	The only place.
EZRA	Dad, I can't do that.
DAD	Go, go, go!
EZRA	I can't. It's dangerous.
DAD	We could blast our way out.
EZRA	Dad, I can't.
DAD	But I don't want to injure innocent people.
EZRA	They're coming. Dad, the ticket collector's coming. Do something.
GUARD	Have I seen your ticket?
EZRA	I… I'm sorry.
GUARD	Are you with somebody?
EZRA	I'm… Then a man said.
MAN	It's all right.

	He's with me.
GUARD	Have you got his ticket sir?
MAN	I've mislaid it. I'll pay for him.
GUARD	Where are you going?
EZRA	Manchester.
GUARD	Don't let it happen again.
MAN	He won't.
EZRA	The guard goes.
MAN	The man looks at him. You'd better sit down.
DAD	Trust no one.
EZRA	Ezra sits down. Thank you.
MAN	Are you running away?
DAD	Trust no one.
EZRA	No. I'm going to see my dad. In Manchester.
MAN	Always travel without a ticket?
DAD	Trust no one.
EZRA	I lost it.
MAN	Why didn't you just say?
EZRA	I thought I might get into trouble.
MAN	The man smiled.
DAD	Trust no one.
MAN	Now why don't I believe a word you say?
EZRA	Ezra stands up to go. Then suddenly The train goes into a tunnel.
	INTERVAL

Part Two

EZRA	September 8th 2003, 11:53
	Ezra's still on the train.
	Dad?
	Dad, where are you?
	We're hiding in the toilet.
	Things I've never seen in stories.
	The goody dying.
	The baddy getting off with girl.
	The baddy winning.
	Have you?
	Or the hero hiding in the toilet.
	Stupid.
DAD	We're not alone.
EZRA	Yes we are.
DAD	No we're not.
EZRA	We are.
DAD	No we're not.
	Look behind you.
EZRA	Ezra turns slowly.
DAD	Mirror Man.
	He draws.
	But too slow.
EZRA	Ezra's not playing.
	He's counting his money
	I don't know if I've got enough left.
	I'll have to get a bus.
DAD	Wait.
	The train's slowing down.
	An ambush.
	Hit the floor.
EZRA	They lie on the floor.

127

It stinks
It stinks really bad.
Dad.
Dad
I can't do this.
They're going to catch me.

September 8th 2003, 11:56
Sorry.
I've got to go home.
That's it then
I know it's rubbish but it'll have to do.
Ezra gives up in the toilet.
The end.
Then comes the announcement.
Manchester.
The next stop is Manchester Piccadilly.
The train terminates here.
Please take all luggage and personal belongings.
We get up and leave the train.
We walk down the platform slowly
We see the woman with the little girl.
She says goodbye.
Then she waves to the driver and points at me.
I wave at him too, and point at her.
We get closer to the barrier.
And then…

MAN	Hallo again.
EZRA	It's the man who paid for me.
MAN	Seen your dad?
DAD	Don't trust him.
EZRA	Not yet. He's a bit late.
MAN	Do you need any help?
DAD	Don't trust him.
EZRA	He looks nice.

	No, thank you.
MAN	You sure?
EZRA	He could be a dad. Yes.
MAN	Suit yourself.
EZRA	The man turned away.
DAD	Well done, Ezra.
EZRA	What do I do now?
DAD	I don't know.
EZRA	You don't know?
DAD	No.
EZRA	Dad, what do I do?
DAD	Find my house?
EZRA	How?
DAD	Don't know.
EZRA	You're useless. I need to ask somebody. Who?
DAD	Any one of them could be an enemy.
EZRA	I've got to ask somebody.
DAD	No.
EZRA	I see the back of the man. He's leaving the station. Mister!
DAD	Trust no one.
EZRA	I've got to trust someone.
DAD	No one.
EZRA	Dad It's stupid. You're just useless. You're a total waste of space.

Shut up.
I need some help.
I turn my back on Dad.
I get out Louise's birthday card.
I walk up to the man.
This address,
Which bus do I get?

MAN   25.
        What's your dad doing letting you run round the
        country on your own?

EZRA   He's at work
        And I'm early.

MAN   Look son.
        Take a bit of advice.
        I don't know what you're doing
        And I don't know where you're going.
        But be careful.
        Not everybody's to be trusted, you know.
        I think you'd better come with me.

EZRA   No.

MAN   Come on.

EZRA   I can't.
        I can't.
        No.

MAN   I think you should.

EZRA   So I ran
        And I kept running

        So I've been on another bus.
        Don't know where Dad is
        Probably on the roof.
        Stupid.
        Now Ezra's standing outside a house.
        I check the birthday card.
        It's the right house.
        I don't know what to do.

Dad?
Dad, where are you?
Dad?
Dad?
Don't leave me now.
Where are you?
Gone?
Not now.
Dad, I need you.
Come back.
I'm on my own
And I don't know how this story's going to end.

September 8th 2003, 13:00
I look at the house.
The curtain twitches.
There's somebody in.
I walk up to the front door.
And I ring the bell.

DAD	Ezra's dad answers the door.
	He's got a mobile in his hand.
	He looks at Ezra.
EZRA	Ezra looks at his dad.
	He opens his mouth.
	Nothing comes out.
DAD	That was quick.
EZRA	Was it?
DAD	Your mum just texted me.
	He holds it out to Ezra.
	Ring her?
EZRA	Shakes his head.
DAD	Dad texts
	He just arrived.
	Well you'd better come in.
EZRA	Ezra goes in.
DAD	Another text.

	Your mum. Of course I'll keep him here. What else would I do with him?
EZRA	Dad's annoyed.
DAD	Sit down.
EZRA	Ezra sits down.
DAD	Dad sits down.
EZRA	Another text.
DAD	Your mum again.
EZRA	Dad texts.
DAD	No. Don't start. He stops. She hasn't changed. He looks at Ezra again. Do you want a drink?
EZRA	What have you got?
DAD	Coffee. Have to be black, I haven't been to the shops.
EZRA	Ezra shakes his head. Don't like coffee.
DAD	Dad looks at Ezra.
EZRA	Ezra looks around the room. The curtains are drawn
DAD	Your mum's got half the police in the country looking for you. She's been worried sick. She'll be here soon. You hungry?
EZRA	Ezra shakes his head. I brought supplies.
DAD	So why did you run away?
EZRA	I didn't.

DAD   What?

EZRA   I didn't run away.
             I came to see you.

DAD   Why?

EZRA   We sit.
             Ezra looks around.
             There isn't much furniture.
             It's very tidy.
             There's just chairs
             A table
             And
             The train set.
             I get the train out.
             I hold it out to him.
             I brought this. You left it.

DAD   It's broken.

EZRA   Can you mend it?

DAD   Doubt it.
             That's why I left it.

EZRA   Do you play with it?

DAD   No.

EZRA   Does it work?

DAD   Yes.

EZRA   Can I see it?

DAD   If you like.

EZRA   Dad switches it on.
             It goes round and round.

DAD   That's it

EZRA   Ezra watches the train.

DAD   You've grown.

EZRA   Ezra doesn't know what to say.

DAD   How's your sister?

EZRA	A pest. She got a new chair.
DAD	Oh? Dad doesn't know what to say.
EZRA	Yeah, it's sweet. Power assisted. She lets me go on it. 'cept it broke down first week she got it. We had to get the AA out. It goes now.
DAD	Good.
EZRA	Is that all it does?
DAD	What else do you want it to do?
EZRA	It just goes round and round.
DAD	Yeah.
EZRA	Mum's got a new boyfriend.
DAD	Has she?
EZRA	We just sat and looked at each other.
DAD	Dad smiled.
EZRA	Ezra didn't.
DAD	What are you looking at?
EZRA	I thought you'd be different.
DAD	Did you?
EZRA	I thought you'd have your uniform on.
DAD	Why?
EZRA	Well, you're a soldier.
DAD	Not any more.
EZRA	You were a hero.
DAD	I'm not. Your mum'll be here soon.
EZRA	Dad?

DAD	What?
EZRA	Why did you go? Were you on a mission?
DAD	A what?
EZRA	A mission. A secret mission you couldn't tell anybody about.
DAD	No.
EZRA	In the war?
DAD	What war?
EZRA	Was it my fault?
DAD	There was a knock at the door. That'll be your mum. I'd better get it.
EZRA	So the door opened
MUM	And there was Mum.
LOUISE	And Louise right behind her.
EZRA	September 8th 2003, 14:00 War broke out.
DAD	Dad stepped back.
LOUISE	Mum didn't look at him.
MUM	Ezra, where the hell have you been? I've been out of my mind with worry. How could you? How could you? Are you alright?
DAD	He just got here.
EZRA	Yes, Mum.
MUM	I've been so worried. I've had the police out.
EZRA	You grassed!
LOUISE	It was Spud.
MUM	What were you thinking of?

EZRA	Mum.
MUM	Or were you thinking at all?
DAD	He came to see me.
LOUISE	Mum ignores him.
DAD	I didn't ask him.
LOUISE	Mum's angry.
MUM	Are you all right? Nobody…
EZRA	Yes, Mum. I'm all right.
MUM	Because there's people… You can't trust…
EZRA	I'm all right.
DAD	He's alright.
LOUISE	Mum doesn't look at him.
DAD	Leave him alone.
LOUISE	Mum doesn't answer.
EZRA	What?
MUM	Home. Now.
EZRA	No.
MUM	Say goodbye to your dad and come.
EZRA	That can't be it. It can't be. It can't end like this.
DAD	Have you got time for a cup of tea?
EZRA	Please, Mum?
MUM	We've got a train to catch.
DAD	There's plenty.
MUM	Alright then.

EZRA	So Dad got the tea.
DAD	Sorry. No milk. I could nip down the corner shop.
MUM	It's alright.
LOUISE	Nobody's saying anything.
MUM	Mum doesn't want to say anything.
DAD	Dad can't think of anything to say.
EZRA	This is nice, isn't it?
LOUISE	No. Well, it's not.
DAD	You're looking well.
EZRA	Dad's talking to you, Mum.
MUM	Thanks.
EZRA	Ezra turns to Louise. See.
MUM	Mum puts the cup down. Thanks for the tea. We'd better go.
EZRA	Already?
MUM	What were you expecting, Ezra?
EZRA	I thought you'd get back together.
LOUISE	Now nobody's saying anything. For a very long time
EZRA	I thought you'd talk to Dad.
LOUISE	Mum still isn't looking at Dad.
MUM	We've got nothing to say to one another.
EZRA	You must have.
MUM	Well I haven't.
LOUISE	That's a bit childish.
MUM	What?

LOUISE	Did I say that out loud?
EZRA	Yes.
LOUISE	Well, you'd never let us get away with that.
MUM	Wouldn't I?
EZRA	No. You're always making us talk when we don't want to.
MUM	This isn't one of your stories Ezra. You can't make this one come out right.
LOUISE	Mum's looking at Ezra But she's shouting at Dad.
DAD	Don't be so hard on him.
MUM	Why's he so interested now?
DAD	He's my son.
MUM	He never cared much while he was there.
DAD	I sent letters.
EZRA	Did you?
MUM	I want to forget about you.
EZRA	Did you?
LOUISE	Did you?
MUM	Like you forgot about us.
EZRA	You sent letters?
DAD	I texted. You never told them?
MUM	Kids need more than letters.
EZRA	You never told us.
MUM	Tell your dad thank you. We've got a train to catch. I'm going to tidy myself up.
EZRA	Mum went out.
DAD	Dad looked at the floor.

LOUISE	Hallo Dad.
DAD	Hallo.
LOUISE	I'm Louise.
DAD	I know. Is that your new chair?
LOUISE	Yes.
DAD	Very nice.
EZRA	Dad. There's something I haven't told you.
DAD	What?
EZRA	I need a kidney transplant I'm going to die if I don't get one. You're the only match.
DAD	What?
EZRA	You've got to give me one of yours. You'll have to come back.
DAD	Your mum never said.
LOUISE	That's because it's not true.
EZRA	It is. I'm dying.
LOUISE	You're lying. He's always doing this. That's what Ezra does. He makes up stories.
DAD	Do you?
EZRA	Sometimes.
LOUISE	All the time.
DAD	What about?
LOUISE	Mum comes back in.
DAD	What about?
EZRA	You!

	I make up stories about you.
LOUISE	Mum's looking at Ezra as if he's a stranger.
EZRA	Come home, Dad. Please come home.
DAD	I can't. Your mum and me. You can see what it's like.
EZRA	She's just angry.
LOUISE	She's hurt.
DAD	It doesn't work.
LOUISE	It won't work.
EZRA	You could make it work.
DAD	Some things can't be mended.
EZRA	Why not? They should be… You can mend it. If anyone can…
DAD	I can't.
EZRA	You can. You're brave. You're not afraid of anything.
MUM	He's afraid of you.
LOUISE	Mum's making it worse.
EZRA	Ezra took out a machine gun and mowed his family down.
LOUISE	Don't be stupid Ez. That won't help.
EZRA	How can he be afraid of me? Afraid of me! I'm just a kid.
DAD	You don't know me at all do you?
EZRA	No, I don't. I had to make you up.
DAD	I was a soldier. But I'm no hero. Didn't Mum say?

MUM   He doesn't need to know.

EZRA   She doesn't like to talk about it.

DAD   I can face a gun.
            But I can't face you.

EZRA   Why not?

DAD   I let you down.

LOUISE   Well you'd better get it sorted now.

MUM   How?

LOUISE   Well, we can't can we?
            We're just kids.

EZRA   Dad looks at Mum.

LOUISE   Well?

DAD   I'm sorry.

MUM   I know.

DAD   We should talk more.

LOUISE   Mum looks at Dad.

EZRA   For the first time.

MUM   I know.

EZRA   Then me and Mum and Louise go for the train.
            We go home.
            I have to talk to the police.
            Dad didn't come home.
            And he never will.
            But the story doesn't end there.
            Or maybe another one starts.
            September 12th 2003, 14:15
            I'm in my room again.
            The curtains are drawn.
            It's a mess.
            No, it really is a mess this time

LOUISE   Louise brings in a parcel.

EZRA   What's that?

LOUISE   A bomb.
           She gives it to him.

EZRA   Where's it from?

LOUISE   A helicopter dropped it.

EZRA   Ezra looks at it.

LOUISE   It's come through the post.

EZRA   I open it.
           There's a mobile phone
           And a message.
           I open the curtains so I can read it.
           It's from my dad.
           I text his number.
           Dad?
           Dad?
           Are you there?
           Hallo.
           Thanks for the phone.
           Yeah, yeah, I will text for a chat.
           Thanks.
           Come and see you?
           I'll have to ask Mum.
           She'll say yes.
           I know she will.
           Love Ezra

LOUISE   Louise kicks him.

EZRA   And Louise.

LOUISE   He sent me a present too.

EZRA   What?

LOUISE   Wheelchair Barbie.

EZRA   Really?
           I didn't know…
           Why are you smiling?

LOUISE   Gotcha.

SPUD   Spud comes in.

	Your mum sent me in.
EZRA	Got a mobile, Dad sent it.
SPUD	Has he completed his mission?
EZRA	No. He's not on a mission. He's just living in Manchester.
SPUD	Are you coming out?
EZRA	Yeah.
SPUD	What?
EZRA	Yeah. How's your mum?
SPUD	She's in the kitchen talking to your mum.
EZRA	What? She came out?
SPUD	Only because she wanted to get that fiver I gave you. She was really angry. She was almost her old self. She's having a cup of tea. She's forgotten the fiver.
EZRA	Let's go before she remembers. Spud, what's a good ending for a story?
SPUD	And they all lived happily ever after.
EZRA	That is so rubbish. So rubbish. No one would ever believe it. So, I'm still working on the end. I'll have to let you know.
LOUISE	Can I come?
EZRA	You are joking I hope. You're my little sister. Here, play with my Action Man.

SPUD   And have a Mars bar.

LOUISE   Ezra and Spud leave the room.
          They don't see the train start to work.
          Or the figure of Dad emerge.
          He's looking at it.
          He stops it.
          He starts to pack it away.

          THE END